Breach of Faith, Breach of Trust

The Story of Lou Ann Soontiens,
Father Charles Sylvestre, and Sexual Abuse
within the Catholic Church

Jim Gilbert

iUniverse, Inc.
New York   Bloomington

Breach of Faith, Breach of Trust
The Story of Lou Ann Soontiens, Father Charles Sylvestre,
and Sexual Abuse within the Catholic Church

Copyright © 2009 Jim Gilbert and Lou Ann Soontiens

All rights reserved. No part of this book may be used or reproduced by any means, graphic, electronic, or mechanical, including photocopying, recording, taping or by any information storage retrieval system without the written permission of the publisher except in the case of brief quotations embodied in critical articles and reviews.

iUniverse books may be ordered through booksellers or by contacting:

iUniverse
1663 Liberty Drive
Bloomington, IN 47403
www.iuniverse.com
1-800-Authors (1-800-288-4677)

Because of the dynamic nature of the Internet, any Web addresses or links contained in this book may have changed since publication and may no longer be valid. The views expressed in this work are solely those of the author and do not necessarily reflect the views of the publisher, and the publisher hereby disclaims any responsibility for them.

ISBN: 978-1-4401-9006-3 (pbk)
ISBN: 978-1-4401-9008-7 (cloth)
ISBN: 978-1-4401-9007-0 (ebook)

Library of Congress Control Number: 2009912948

Printed in the United States of America

iUniverse rev. date: 4/9/10

This book is dedicated to Lou Ann's husband, Frank Soontiens, her two sons (Wayne and Chris Chandler), her daughter-in-law Kelly, as well as her counselor Connie Coatsworth and her lawyer Rob Talach. Without the support of these people, Lou Ann's story might have had a much different ending.

Contents

Acknowledgments		ix
Introduction		xi
Chapter One	A Brief History of Clergy Sexual Abuse within the Early Catholic Church	1
Chapter Two	An Overview of Clergy Sexual Abuse within the Modern Catholic Church	8
Chapter Three	From a Trickle to a Flood	12
Chapter Four	Lou Ann's Story	22
Chapter Five	God or Someone Could Have or Should Have Stopped Him	48
Chapter Six	Sylvestre the Molester	57
Chapter Seven	Victims, Villains, and Heroes	72
Chapter Eight	Restoring the Faith in the Catholic Church	90
Conclusion		101
The Final Word		107

Acknowledgments

The author would like to gratefully acknowledge the following people for their help in the creation of this book. Jim Blake and the *Chatham Daily News,* Sun Media as well as the *Windsor Star* (cover photo). Lisa Gilbert for her tireless efforts in editing some difficult material. Paul and Annie Gilbert for their insights and Sheila Gibbs for her research assistance and sage advice.

Introduction

Let the little children come to me, and do not stop them; for it is to such as these that the kingdom of heaven belongs.
Matthew 19:14 (NRSV)

In *Sexual Abuse within the Catholic Church*, Michael Bland states:

> To protect ourselves from the horror of clerical sexual abuse, we all imagine or believe that, IF sexual abuse does occur, it happens in another city, in a different social class or to individuals who are, somehow, not like us. (1)

The citizens who live within the bounds of the Diocese of London (Windsor, Chatham, London, Sarnia, St. Thomas, and so forth) can no longer pretend that these things only happen in other places. We know they happen to the girl down the street and the family we once knew. We know a man whom many trusted, revered, and never suspected committed them. Now that we know that they happen here, we must face them and hopefully react to them.

I did not want to write this book. After all, I am basically a social historian who tends to write tributes to the history of towns, rivers, and cities. In general, I celebrate the deeds of local movers and shakers. I may have occasionally dealt briefly with the misdeeds of others, but rarely did I take the time or feel the need to dwell on the lives of those considered to be much less than heroic in much detail. I enjoy looking at interesting people, the roles they played, and how they figured into the big picture. My themes are typically upbeat, inspiring, uplifting, and rarely without some kind of hope.

I may have sometimes deplored the action (or lack of action) of certain groups or individuals in history, but never did I deal with such a situation where there was so much pain, so much sorrow, and such a complete loss of trust and faith in an institution and its leaders. Before I began, I was not even sure if I really believed if this kindly old man, who I had seen briefly on the television and in newspapers as the story developed, had really sexually abused all these women. Probably like many others, I privately postulated that these women saw a way of making a fast buck from the supposedly riches-laden, much-beleaguered Catholic Church. They did not mind putting an octogenarian priest through hell to get it.

I was baptized in the Catholic Church. I made my first communion, and I was confirmed. I was even married in the Catholic Church. Over the years, I had become what is best described as a "lapsed Catholic." In my earlier, idealistic years, I had intellectual disagreements with the church, ironically enough, often over the way women were treated and their secondary role in the church. But I maintained a great deal of respect for the Catholic Church. Any time that an outsider would attack it, I would vehemently defend it on those areas that I could without compromising my position.

Then I received a phone call from Lou Ann Soontiens. She wanted me to help her write her story. She stated she wanted to clearly tell what had happened to her at the hands of Father Sylvestre over the course of several years.

She must have anticipated my reluctance to do so because she was quickly able to list all the reasons why she firmly felt I should be the one to recount her story. "I've been following your newspaper columns over the years, and I like your personal writing style," she said. "I respect your views on various aspects of social history. A lot of people told me that you have a strong sense of social justice and that you're an advocate for the underdog."

Although I was impressed with her passion to have her story told and flattered by the obvious research that she had done on me, I still politely demurred, citing a hundred reasons why I was not suited for such a daunting task.

I tried to suggest that possibly a book on such a topic would not be a good idea. I hoped the tone of my words did not hint at my skepticism, but I was not sure. I suggested other approaches and tried to steer her away from what I perceived to be a needless and, to my mind, embarrassing, public statement.

I suppose I was one of those who simply wanted her to forgive, forget, and move on with her life. I look back upon that time now and realize how little I knew and how heartlessly cavalier I could be with another person's life. She would not be deterred. She persevered until I agreed to at least listen to what she had to say.

On a chilly fall day when the warmth of the summer was fading fast and winter's cold reality was hurrying near, I sat down and listened to her unabridged tale for the first time. She told it in such a unemotional manner that it made the gravity of her tale even more sinister, devastating, and shocking. I was not prepared for what she told me, but I knew she was telling me the truth. I was shocked. I was angered and moved. I could feel the tears welling up in my eyes. I did not know if they were tears of anger or compassion. In retrospect, I know that they were both.

She had been living with this truth since she was an innocent child of twelve. She had her innocence stolen from her at such an early age that the pain and suffering within her had become part of her and colored all she did and all she had become. A blatant act of power that she had no control over had shaped, manipulated, and influenced her schooling, career, marriages, and very existence.

After I went away from my first meeting with Lou Ann, I started to read and educate myself about a topic in which I was woefully ignorant. I soon came to realize that sexual abuse within the Catholic Church was not new. It had a long history and involved thousands of victims. It was, in its own horrible fashion, very much an aspect of history that needed to be examined and brought to life. In fact, I came to understand that the sexual abuse of children was not new nor totally confined to religious institutions. It existed anywhere that children were placed in positions where they lacked power.

In my mind, Lou Ann became a symbol of not only those other forty-six local victims, but the countless others, both girls and boys, throughout time and throughout the world, who had suffered, not only at the hands of offending clerics, but abusive, power-wielding adults in all professions.

I felt embarrassed and angry with myself for making the same assumption that many parents, teachers, and fellow clergy had made over the last fifty years. Kindly, supportive, understanding Father Sylvestre would never have done that. These girls must be mistaken. Maybe it was mass hysteria or the power of suggestion, like the young girls who accused others of being witches at Salem. We all make excuses in our minds to deal with situations that seem too horrible and too unthinkable to really examine.

Writing a book to make others aware of their pain and suffering and help in the healing process of Lou Ann and the other victims seemed like the very least I could do. In the whole scope of things, it may be a rather small and insignificant gesture, but something in my gut told me that it was the right thing to do. In light of the pain and suffering that the victims of a master sexual predator endured, I soon realized I had a task I may not like, but it was one that needed to be done.

This book is not a mindless rant against the Catholic Church. Enemies of the church will not find ammunition here to destroy this centuries-old, venerable institution. The reader will find stories from near and far that clearly demonstrate a history of, at best, poor decisions, and, at worst, calculated decisions designed to save face. No one can be without sympathy for the hierarchy of the Catholic Church trying to deal with countless abhorrent situations; but, at the same time, I think we all agree that there had to be better, more efficient, and more Christian ways of dealing with a problem that has arisen so many times within the priesthood.

The stories recounted in this examination are not always pleasant, but, after all is said and done, the hope is real. That is the one thing that all of us, Catholics and non-Catholics alike, can agree. Sexual abuse is not the sole property of the Catholic Church and a small minority of its priests. We must all be aware of this ugly part of life, and it forces all of us to be vigilant in protecting and preserving the innocence of all children. The tales need to be told; we all need to listen. We can no longer close our ears and pretend they do not exist. We, as a collective society, have all done that for much too long.

There must be hope for the victims as they commence their long road toward recovery, just as there must be hope for the rejuvenation of a church desperately needing new visions, directions, and approaches. All of these must be based on serious and difficult examinations of where the Catholic Church has been and where it is going. It also, of necessity, will depend on new players not usually given power within the church to step forward and play meaningful, thoughtful, and innovative roles. If the many victims of Father Sylvestre and thousands of others throughout the world can endure what they have for so long and begin anew, then the Catholic Church should be able to do so as well.

You will not like all that you read in this examination. Some will make you angry; some will make you upset. Some may very well make you cry, but you cannot help but be somewhat moved by its contents. Your heart will reach out to Lou Ann when you read her brave words. She refused to temper, modify, or couch these words in vague phrases. She tells things exactly the way they occurred in its entire graphic and terrible context.

Like many other victims of sexual abuse, she wants all of us to be very clear about what actually happened. They want us to know, feel, and, to the best of our limited abilities, understand. All have had to hide a terrible secret for much of their lives. Now they are freed from these horrible shackles, they want to try to communicate the depth of the pain, anguish, and guilt they have felt for so long.

In many ways, they must feel like Lazarus coming back from the dead to tell us all what it was like. We have a duty to listen and attempt to understand, despite the fact that a deep, true understanding is probably well beyond our capabilities. No matter how impossible, we must at least make the attempt. After all, a good definition of true intelligence is one that purports the theory that we never forsake attempting to achieve that which we fully understand is impossible.

Conservative Catholics may not always agree with my comments, suggestions, or observations. That is not only acceptable, but extremely desirable. It is a time for examination, dissent, argument, and thoughtful consideration. It is not a time to ignore these things in the hope they will disappear. We, as a society, have done that for much too long, and they have neither gone away nor improved on their own.

Regardless of how you react and feel and what you take away from this book, I hope it will make you stop and think. I hope it not only makes you pause and reflect, but also discuss and, hopefully, in the final analysis, be moved to feel, care, and act. Maybe no one else in the future will need to write a book about a topic that none of us wants to even imagine.

Endnotes

1) Bland, M.J. (2001). "The Psychological and Spiritual Effects of Child Abuse When The Perpetrator Is A Catholic Priest". Disertation Abstyracts International, 2002.

Chapter One

A Brief History of Clergy Sexual Abuse within the Early Catholic Church

Any sexual abuse perpetrated by adults on children or adolescents entrusted to their care, is a serious moral offense. The offense is compounded by the scandalous harm done to the physical and moral integrity of the young, who will remain scarred by it, all their lives; and the violation of responsibility for their upbringing.
Catechism of the Catholic Church (1994)

Vatican II corrupted the institution of the church. Look at its main fruits: dwindling members and pedophilia.
Mel Gibson, as quoted in *Time,* January 27, 2003

Many traditional, conservative Catholics are under the impression that the Second Vatican Council, with all of its liberal views, created a climate that somehow encouraged priests to assume the role of sexual predators. Although this view can be used to explain away any number of real and imagined unpleasant things happening in the church and society, the primary goals of Vatican II were to reach out to the world as a whole and move the Catholic Church into a position to better deal with the twentieth century and beyond.

Critics of Vatican II insist this movement did little else but make Catholics, including its priests, more secular. In their eyes, the world did not become more Catholic, but church members simply became worldlier in the worst sense of that term.

Following this train of thought, Catholics, like Mel Gibson, conclude that the seemingly large number of incidents of *pedophilia* (sexual encounters with children) and *ephebophilia* (sexual encounters with younger adolescents) reported among priests is purely a modern phenomenon and things like this never happened in the "good old days of Catholicism."

However, a closer examination of the historical facts reveals that this view is quite inaccurate. Abuse by Catholic priests was actually occurring long before the start of Vatican II (1962–1965). Although mandatory celibacy among Catholic clerics did not come into existence until the twelfth century at the Second Lateran Council of 1139, a number of the leaders within the Roman Catholic Church had been advocating for it since the fourth century.(2)

The push for celibacy among priests was partially in reaction to the many incidents of priests being accused of adultery, homosexuality, and child abuse. The theory may very well have been that, if a priest takes a vow of celibacy, these errant behaviors would be controlled or significantly reduced. It was a noble thought, but one that doesn't fit reality. It was a medieval view of life. The fact that this anachronistic concept has survived so long without change is remarkable and disturbing. Some critics believe it is a possible reason for aberrant sexual behavior among clerics.

Support for this view appears in one of the earliest recorded deliveries of church legislation at the Council of Elvira, Spain, in 306 AD. Nearly half of the canons passed at this convocation dealt with aberrant sexual behavior of one kind or another and included penalties levied upon clerics who had fornicated, committed adultery, and committed sexual acts with young boys. (3)

The Catholic hierarchy considered this latter act to be extremely despicable. According to Canon 18 of the Council of Elvira:

> Bishops, presbyters and deacons, if—once placed in the ministry—they are discovered to be sexual offenders, shall not receive communion, not even in the end, because of the scandal and the heinousness of the crime.(4)

Although the Council of Elvira was held in Europe (Spain), this did not mean it was only in Europe where sexual misdeeds were an issue. Convocations of bishops throughout the entire Christian world (Western Europe, Northern Africa, the Middle East, and the British

Isles) held similar meetings shortly after the Spain meetings and passed strict laws in an attempt to "eradicate clerical concubinage, clerical fornication and homosexual activity."(5)

Another source of early Catholic Church history is the recording of individual confessions by priests in Irish monasteries that began in the latter sixth century and continued until the twelfth century. These penitential books list the various acts that the church considered to be sinful. They also provide guidance on the acceptable penance to be imposed.

Several of these penitential books make specific reference to sexual crimes committed by clergy against young boys and girls. The Penitential of Bede (England, eighth century) advises that clerics who commit sodomy with young boys be given increasingly severe penances commensurate with their rank with the higher ranking (bishops) receiving harsher penalties. Due to the number of times reference is made to sex acts in this document, the problem was clearly not isolated. In fact, it was commonly known about in the community and was treated more severely than similar acts committed by laymen.(6)

In 1051, a reform-minded Benedictine monk, St. Peter Damian, a rising star in the Catholic Church (monk, archbishop, and then cardinal), attempted to write how he felt the Catholic Church of the day should deal with what he saw as the widespread sexual abuse committed by the clergy. Although these unclean acts performed by a decadent clergy were generally accepted as the norm, Damian felt it should be stopped immediately. In order to accomplish this reformation, he submitted his document, *The Book of Gomorrah*, to Pope Leo IX.(7)

Damian was adamant that the church had been far too lenient in the past on its clergy who had been involved in sexual crimes and this permissive attitude should cease immediately. He advised Pope Leo to weed out those offenders and deal with them quickly and effectively.

The pope's reaction to the *Book of Gomorrah* would lay out the pattern of response of the Roman Catholic hierarchy even into modern times. He agreed wholeheartedly with Damian and praised him for his reforming nature. He did not disagree with any of his allegations, but he resisted taking decisive action and rooting those sexual offenders out of the clergy. He decided instead to take action only against those who had offended repeatedly and over a long period.(8)

As in recent times, the emphasis was placed not on the impact that these priestly improprieties had on the many victims, as Damian had stressed that the pope should consider, but rather focused on the sinfulness of the clerics and their need to simply admit their past crimes and repent. As we shall see with Father Sylvestre and countless other clerics accused with sexual molestation, once the cleric in question had promised to not do it again, he was allowed to continue his priestly duties in much the same manner he had previously. Penances were vaguely physical. Spiritual punishments did little to change the cleric's behavior.

During the Fourth Lateran Council (1215) and Council of Basle (1449), reformers lashed out at church officials within the Catholic Church who allowed clerics to get away with crimes of a sexual nature. Both of these councils made it clear that vices among priests could not be stopped unless their superiors played an integral role. The canon from the Fourth Lateran Council plainly stated that any "prelate who dares support such in their iniquities, especially in view of money or other temporal advantages, shall be subject to a like punishment."(9)

In fact, in some ways, during the medieval period, the Roman Catholic Church acted more decisively than in contemporary times in dealing with those clerics who abused their vows of celibacy. During this period, church officials sometimes took the view that celibacy violations were not only matters of religion, but also ones that had an impact upon society as a whole. Therefore, after being duly punished by church tribunals, the accused were occasionally turned over to secular authorities for additional prosecution and punishment, which was often harsh and could result in execution.

The Protestant reformers of the sixteenth century (Luther, Zwingli, and Calvin) also saw this problem of sexual transgressions among the clergy as a serious one. At least one reformer described the situation in the following rather graphic and explicit terms:

> [T]he sexual habits of some priests within the Catholic Church result in it becoming a sewer of iniquity, a scandal to the laity and a threat of damnation to the clergy themselves.(10)

In fact, Luther, Calvin, and Zwingli unanimously rejected the notion of mandatory celibacy for their clergy in the Reformation movement, largely because of the seriousness of this issue of sexual impropriety that they had witnessed in the Catholic Church.

The Protestant Reformation created a number of shock waves within the Catholic Church. Many within the church wanted immediate sweeping, radical changes. The Council of Trent (1545–1563) was convened as a result. However, while many radical reforms were adopted, the proposal that would allow priests to marry was dismissed. Mandatory celibacy was reinforced. Catholic leaders of the time held up celibacy as a situation superior in all facets to marriage. One can speculate that priests would remain celibate to possibly separate them from the Reformers, who could be pictured as obsessed by such worldly concerns as sex. Once again, we see a concept full of noble intentions, but totally lacking in a sense of what had happened in the past and the understanding of human sexuality.

Attempts were made at the Council of Trent to enact laws that would curb celibacy violations among its clerics and prevent such transgressions through a series of mandatory training and education for priests. However, the bishops at Trent were no more successful at preventing deviant sexual behavior among their priests than any other Catholic council had been in the past. Illicit sex with women, men, and young boys continued, albeit in a little more discreet manner.(11) The Roman Catholic Church had apparently not yet come to terms with its dirty little secret. I suppose some might argue that little has changed in today's world.

From this admittedly very brief and cursory history of the early (306 AD to seventeenth century) Roman Catholic Church's treatment of its sexually aberrant clergy, it can be clearly seen that there has always been a number of priests who somehow violated the mandatory celibacy that the Roman Catholic Church imposed on them. It is impossible to determine the actual percentage of the clergy who, at any time in history, participated in acts of sexual impropriety, let alone how many of them were involved in sexual abuse of children. But it is certain that this is not just a modern problem.

Throughout the early history of the Catholic Church, there was, as there is today, a feeling among many people of all faiths that, if priests were only allowed to marry, many of the sexual problems that the clergy experienced would be solved. Obviously, if there were not mandatory celibacy, priests who were involved in monogamous, married relationships would not be in any violation of church canons. However, the belief that this would also put a stop to most molestation of children by priests is a tenuous theory and, as we shall examine later, one that is not generally supported by experts.

One aspect we can glean from the early history of the Catholic Church is that, almost from the very beginning, the church hierarchy developed the attitude of ignoring, excusing, and avoiding issues related to sexual wrongdoings by their clerics. The priests' true problems were misunderstood; the victims' suffering and pain were largely ignored. This attitude among Catholic authorities is one that we will unfortunately come back to repeatedly in this examination. There are very few examples in the early history of the Catholic Church where the leaders within the Catholic Church demonstrated a socially responsible attitude toward sexual crimes committed by their priests.(12)

The real crime of sexual abuse among the clergy is not simply one of a minority of sexually dysfunctional clerics. Rather, it is the total unwillingness of the Roman Catholic hierarchy throughout its history to recognize, understand, and effectively deal with the problem.

Endnotes

2) Thomas Doyle . "A Very Short History of Clergy Sexual Abuse In The Cathoilc Church". Crusade Against Clergy Abuse. Date of Electronic Publication: March 2004. Date Accessed: March 12, 2007.
<http://www.crusadeagainstclergyabuse.com/htm/Ashorthistory.htm>

3) Boswell, John. Christianity, Social Tolerance and Homosexuality. (Chicago: University of Chicago Press, 1980) : 42

4) Doyle, " A Very Short History..."

5) Pierre Payer. Sex And The Penitentials (Toronto: University of Toronto Press, 1984) : 34.

6) Pierre Payer. The Book of Gomorrah (Waterloo, ON, Wilfred Laurier University, 1982) : 6.

7) Perre Payer . The Book of Gomorrah : 7

8) Canon II, 3rd Lateran Council in H. J. Schroeder, editor, Disciplinary Decrees of the General Councils. (St. Louis: B. Herder Book Co., 1997) :224.

9) Elizabeth Abbot. A Short History of CElibacy. (Cambridge, Da Capo Press, 1999):108-113.

10) Canon II, 3rd Lateran Council. :182

11) Thomas Doyle. "A Very Short History..."

12) Thomas Doyle. "A Very Short History...."

Chapter Two

An Overview of Clergy Sexual Abuse within the Modern Catholic Church

The official church and its clergy are masters at show. We regularly put on elaborate liturgies to commemorate everything from papal coronations to earthquakes ... but they cannot be a substitute for authentic pastoral action.
Thomas Doyle, *What Bishops Can Do to Help*

The first chapter provided strong evidence that clergy sexual abuse has been a well-documented and ongoing aspect of life within the Catholic Church since Emperor Constantine officially recognized the church in the early fourth century.

Roman Catholic priests are not the only men of the cloth who abuse children. Clergy of all faiths are guilty of sexual misconduct with both children and adults. Although not nearly enough research has been done in this area, a quick survey of the research that has been conducted reveals certain key points.

Almost 42 percent of respondents in a 1990 study on sexual harassment in the United Methodist Church reported unwanted sexual behavior by a colleague or pastor. This included 17 percent of laywomen who stated their own pastor had harassed them. Also in 1990, a national survey of mainly Protestant pastors by a group at the Center for Ethics and Social Policy, Graduate Theological Union, in Berkeley, California, discovered that about 10 percent of those surveyed had been sexually active with an adult parishioner.(13)

Although scientific, irrefutable data on such matters is impossible to accurately obtain, it can be speculated with some degree of certainty that the percentage of pastors in all religions who sexually abuse children is in the 4–7 percent range. This, by the way, is the same percentage as the incidence of molesters in the general public.(14)

If the prevalence of sexual predators in all religions and all of society is approximately equal, why does the Catholic Church and its pastors seem to receive an undue amount of negative attention? Possibly the answer lies in how the Catholic Church has treated the victims of these sexual crimes throughout its history.

In the early church, victims assumed the leadership within the early Catholic Church would immediately come to their aid. These largely uneducated members of the early Catholic Church thought the church's legal system (canon law) would quickly dispense punishment to the offending priests, victims would be properly cared for, and the offenders would not be allowed to continue their pastoral duties within the church.

However, as we saw earlier, the response by the early church seems to have a great deal in common with the modern-day Catholic Church. Church leaders routinely responded to the problem by attempting to intimidate victims, hoping they could be forced into silence. If silence was not forthcoming, religious leaders within the church stonewalled, deceived, and threatened victims.(15) Many victims of Father Sylvestre would probably find much to share with early victims from over a thousand years ago.

This pattern of response (or rather non-response) to those victims sexually abused by priests continued throughout the next fifteen centuries with very few exceptions. In 1917, the Catholic Church issued a promulgation to all of its bishops in the world, but it was otherwise wrapped in absolute secrecy. This promulgation, like the future ones to be issued in 1922, 1962, 1983, and 2001, was meant to provide special procedures for processing various types of clergy sexual abuse.(16)

The 1962 updated version of the 1917 and 1922 promulgations is interesting because, although it was distributed in the usual manner (to all bishops throughout the world), this particular one was preceded by a papal order, which directed recipients of the document to keep it in the secret archives and not publish nor comment upon it in any manner.

Compared to previous documents dealing with sexual abuse among the clergy issued by the Vatican, this particular one (1962) reveals a clearly defined church policy for dealing with sexual crimes committed by the clergy. (17) Some of the highlights include:

Tribunal and other church personnel are obliged to maintain total and perpetual secrecy. The church's highest degree of confidentially, the Secret of the Holy Office, binds them. Those who violate this secrecy are automatically excommunicated. The absolution or lifting of this excommunication is reserved to the pope himself.

The accuser and witnesses are obliged to take the oath of secrecy. While the threat of excommunication is not attached to the document, the official conducting the prosecution could, at his own discretion, threaten accusers and witnesses with excommunication if they break secrecy.

Anonymous accusations are not automatically ruled out, although they are generally to be rejected.

The document also defined sex crimes as those that included homosexual acts between clerics and members of their own sex, bestiality, and sexual acts of any kind with children. Children are defined in this document with the Latin term *impuberibus* (before the age of reason), defined by church canon as one sixteen years of age or under. Some critics reading this document have great trouble in determining as to whom the crimes apply. Sex crimes are clearly defined as sex with children, sex with males of any age, and all animals, but some readers of the document are confused as to whether sex with young girls is clearly listed as a sex crime or not. The wording, at best, is very confusing.

No matter how confusing some of the points in this document are, some other aspects register very clearly. This 1962 document makes it very clear that the Catholic Church desires at all costs to maintain the highest degree of secrecy and the strictest degree of security about the clergy's worst sexual crimes. Unaddressed in this document is any specific reference to how the victims' issues should be sensitively and effectively addressed. No realization is made in this document of the degree of trauma these sexual crimes committed by the clergy caused and the role the church hierarchy played in this tragedy. By the time the modern era arrived, the Roman Catholic Church had established a rather callous and rather un-Christian method of dealing with the many victims of clergy abuse.

It refused to allow them to speak, grieve, and find inner peace, although many needed to do so more than anything else. By this time in its history, the church should have been ready to become the voice of molested children, but it chose to ignore, patronize, belittle, or discredit them. It refused to walk a mile in the shoes of these children and become their advocates, saviors, and counselors, as one might expect from such an organization.

By the dawn of the 1980s, after all of its painful and embarrassing experiences, the Roman Catholic Church should have been prepared to effectively, professionally, expeditiously, and sensitively deal with all sexual misdeeds that its clergy committed.

When twelve-year-old Scott Gastal took the stand in southwestern Louisiana on the morning of February 6, 1986, to testify against Father Gilbert Gauthe, it began a maelstrom within the Catholic Church that must have seemed to be a precursor to Hurricane Katrina.

Endnotes

13) Anne Simpkinson. "Soul; Betrayal", Beliefnet Inc. Date of Electronic Publication: May 11, 2006. Date Accessed: July 23, 2007. <http://www.beliefnet.com/story/101/story 10199.htm>

14) Stephen J. Rosetti. "The Catholic Church and Child Secxual Abuse". America, The National Catholic Weekly Magazine. Date of Electronic Publication: April 22, 2002. Date Accessed: Feb. 11, 2007. <http//www.catholicbookclub.net>

15) Thomas Doyle. "A Very Short History Of Clergy Sexual Abuse In The Catholic Church". Crusade Against Clergy. Date of Electronic Publication: March 2004. Date Accessed: March 12, 2007.
<http://www.Crusade againstclergyabuse.com/htm/ashorthistory.htm>

16) Thomas Doyle. "A Very Short History..."

17) Thomas Doyle. "A Very Short History..."

Chapter Three

From a Trickle to a Flood

Eventually, the problem will end up on each diocese's steps. One can act now ... Or wait until forced to act. Either way, the time will come.
Stephen J. Rossetti, *A Tragic Grace*

The large Catholic population that resides in the sultry bayous of Louisiana listened in shock as they, as well as the rest of North America, heard for the first time in public the graphic story that twelve-year-old Scott Gastal told. In painful hushed sentences, the young lad described in shocking detail the perversions of a former trusted clergy who systematically sexually abused at least thirty-seven young boys over a period of years.

No matter how shocking and graphic the description of how Father Gilbert Gauthe sodomized the young lad was, it almost paled in comparison when the truth about how the Catholic Church handled Gauthe and his problem over the years became known.

Subsequent investigations revealed the entire community had been kept in the dark about the priest. The church had failed to notify anyone in the parish that Father Gauthe had a long history of sexually abusing children that dated back several years. It failed to let anyone know that the dynamic, young pastor had caused the church to pay out an average of $450,000 to nine families of sexually abused children.(18)

No one knew because the church, although paying out almost $4 million, admitted no liability. It had the cases sealed and made sure there would be no publicity. If it had been left to the Catholic Church, no one would have ever found out, save for the victims, that Father Gauthe, over his clerical career, had raped several other children besides Scott Gastal—and he was active in child pornography distribution.

The Gastal family refused to be silenced or swayed by the threat of excommunication. They were adamant that the world should know about Father Gilbert Gauthe, who had been sentenced to twenty years of hard labor. More importantly, they wanted to expose the mistakes that the church made in dealing with sexual offenders.

Although suffering at the hands of other Catholics who verbally taunted them as traitors, the Gastals managed to pry open the long-locked doors of Catholic deception and expose the injustices. It was in no way an easy battle. The church used every cruel tactic and uncharitable strategy to belittle, intimidate, and destroy the Gastals. They would follow this pattern several times in the future.

Brought about because of their deep feelings of betrayal engendered by their trusted church, their persistence eventually paid off. For the first time, the world saw how church leaders had responded to the complaints of abuse by repeatedly transferring the offender to another parish.

The world also witnessed how Catholic leaders attempted to pass off Gauthe as an anomaly, as "just one priest out of fifty-eight thousand." But their protests lost any credibility when, less than a month after Gauthe's imprisonment, five Native American sisters filed suit against another priest, Father John Engbers, a priest in the same diocese as Gauthe.

The Gastal family, poor, devout Catholics, screamed their hurt, anger, and frustration with the Catholic Church from the backwater bayous of Cajun Louisiana. After hundreds and hundreds of years of victims' cries fell upon deaf ears, the world heard them and responded.

In the 1970s, there averaged approximately twelve thousand complaints a year concerning sexual abuse among the general population. By the mid-1980s, there were over one hundred and fifty thousand complaints filed with reference to Roman Catholic clergy. Police estimated that a mere 8 percent of these reports were lacking in credibility.(19)

Within the Catholic community of North America, the trickle of complaints filed against Catholic clergy for sexual crimes grew from a trickle to a virtual flood. After the court case in Louisiana, victims were encouraged to think of themselves as courageous survivors who wanted to heal their wounds in public. They wanted the world to know about how they were sexually used and abused by, not only the clergy, but also parents, relatives, teachers, supervisors, and a host of other predators. They no longer wanted to suffer in silence. They wanted to be recognized as survivors. Many of those abused by Catholic clergy hoped the church, now so openly exposed, would be anxious to make amends, seek to repair the damage done to the growing number of victims, and make sure that such things would not happen again.

Most bishops in North America refused to admit there was a problem. They insisted, once again, that priest molesters were simply an aberration and there were simply not enough of them to rate concern or actions. They felt it was an overreaction that the media, Protestants, and other "Catholic bashers" created. They said the world would soon come to its senses.

However, the situation did not subside, nor did the number of complaints ease. Instead, throughout the next three decades, the specter of sexual misdeeds by Catholic clergy surfaced repeatedly at an alarming rate. The victims of Father Sylvestre, quietly concealed in the deceptively innocent farming communities of southwestern Ontario, were far from being alone in their pain and suffering.

In 1985, Father Carmelo Baltazar of Boise, Idaho, was finally indicted, convicted, and sentenced to seven years in prison, but this was only after three different dioceses had removed him for sexual misconduct with minors. Even when Baltazar was accused of fondling a boy from his parish, who was in double-leg traction at a Boise hospital, no action was taken to address the crime.(20)

In 1989, within the Archdiocese of New York, Father Daniel Calabrese was moved from parish to parish and progressively given better positions even though there had been persistent complaints about his sexual misdeeds with young boys. Parents complained that Father Calabrese would show pornographic movies to teenage boys after giving them alcohol. Calabrese was eventually charged with sodomizing a sixteen-year-old boy, whom he had gotten drunk on vodka.(21)

In Orlando, Florida, Father William Authenreith got away with molesting young boys for more than a decade. Whenever there was a complaint of a sexual nature, the church would simply transfer him to another parish. When one father complained to a church official, the official haughtily replied, "It is not for you to judge. That's for God to do." In 1985, Authenreith's perverse sexual odyssey ended when so many lawsuits piled up against the Catholic clergyman that his behavior could no longer be ignored.(22)

When Father Jude McGeough arrived in 1977 at the parish of Father William O'Connell in Bristol, Rhode Island, to serve as his assistant, he found the entire town knew of O'Connell's love of boozing and fondness for the company of teenage boys. When McGeough complained to his superiors in Providence, nothing was done. When he prepared a well-documented, four-page report on O'Connell's unpriestly lifestyle and submitted it to church officials, no action was taken. In frustration, McGeough sought a transfer to another parish. Parishioners continued to complain to Bishop Angell about O'Connell. Another priest actually witnessed a young boy, dressed in only bikini underwear, cavorting in the rectory. However, it was not until February 1985 that Father O'Connell was arrested, charged, and convicted of twenty-six counts of sexual contact with three boys and sentenced to a single year in jail.(23)

In 1988–1989, the Royal Commission of Inquiry in Canada conducted an investigation of abuse charges at the Mount Cashel Orphanage in Newfoundland. Several Christian Brothers at this institution were accused of physically and sexually abusing schoolboys over a number of years. The final judgment of the Hughes Inquiry resulted in twenty-three of the Brothers being charged. Nine were convicted of sexually assaulting at least eighty-one victims. The investigation also came to what was becoming a very common conclusion concerning sexual abuse within the church. In an attempt to cover up the abuse at Mount Cashel, the Catholic Church leaders continued to play the shell game of moving Brothers anytime complaints started to reach a crisis level. It was also concluded that the archdiocesan leadership were aware of this abuse since at least the mid-1970s and did nothing to stop it or come to the aid of the victims.(24)

In 1992, Father Kevin Michael Rolston from British Columbia was convicted of gross indecency and buggery of three young boys in Kelowna. The presiding judge described his testimony during the trial as being "glib," "insincere," and "crafted to suit his convenience."(25)

Bishop Hubert O'Connor resigned his position as bishop of Prince George, British Columbia, after being accused of taking eight women from their homes, forcing them to attend church school, and then sexually abusing them. At the time, O'Connor was principal of a Native residential school near Williams Lake in the 1960s.(26)

Father John Geoghan of the Archdiocese of Boston was sentenced to ten years imprisonment in 2002 for molesting an estimated two hundred children over a thirty-three-year period from 1962 to 1995. The Catholic Church is expected to pay up to $45 million when all the suits in this case have been addressed.(27)

Father Rudolph Kos, of Dallas, Texas, was sentenced to life imprisonment for abusing eleven boys in All Saints' Catholic Church from 1981 to 1992. The Texas court system ordered the Diocese of Dallas to pay $119.6 million to the families of the eleven boys. At the time, it was considered to be "the largest verdict ever awarded against the Catholic Church."(28)

In what should have been a loud wake-up call to congregations and the local church hierarchy, the Diocese of London faced a messy sexual abuse lawsuit in the late 1960s and early 1970s. Brothers John, Ed, and Gary Swales and their family sought damages for pain and suffering they said resulted from abuse by Father Barry Glendinning when they were students of his at St. Peter's Seminary. The boys, aged six to ten at the time of the assaults, told stories of how Father Glendinning would ply them with liquor and dirty songs before he abused them.(29)

In 1974, Glendinning was convicted of six acts of gross indecency. The Diocese of London paid $1.3 million to the Swales family, but this was not before the Diocese of London attempted to countersue ten-year-old John Swales, claiming he was being dishonest in a few of his responses.(30)

In a surprising and almost unprecedented move, the Swales family also attempted to sue the Vatican, claiming that Rome was responsible for the maintenance of a uniform set of rules and principles that collectively define the ideology of the Roman Catholic religion as well as the teaching and training of their priests. Although the suit failed, it should have sent a warning message to the Diocese of London and entire Roman Catholic Church.

In the trial, it was revealed, after reports about his abusive behavior with young boys at St. Peter's began circulating, Father Glendinning was treated for alcoholism and then transferred to the Edmonton

Theological College, where he, once again, began to molest young boys.(31)

When the abuse claims against Father Sylvestre began to surface more than two decades later, the Diocese of London had obviously not learned anything about the proper way to deal with their sexually abusing priests.

The preceding examples are only the tip of a very large and dark iceberg. Between 1980 and 2002, it was reported that over eight hundred priests in the United States (at least sixty in Canada) had been through the court process for sexual misdeeds. Thirteen hundred priests had been treated for psychosexual disorders; at least two hundred and fifty priests had been removed of their pastoral duties.(32)

Four bishops had resigned, one priest was murdered by an alleged victim, and at least two priests committed suicide after being accused of abuse. It was also reported that abuse allegations had surfaced in more than 95 percent of the one hundred and ninety-four American Catholic dioceses during that same period.(33)

But it is also important to keep in mind that there are over fifty thousand Catholic priests in the United States and eleven thousand priests in Canada who have never been charged with any sexual crimes. It is sometimes very easy, with the rash of cases being processed currently and the large media attention placed upon these pastoral sexual crimes in North America, to forget that the vast majority of priests are sensitive, compassionate, religious individuals who have given up all worldly pursuits in order to dedicate their lives to serving God and helping others.

It is also important to keep in mind that, while clergy pedophilia and ephebophilia are the sexual crimes that capture the headlines and occupy the minds of the media, 80–90 percent of the cases revolving around clergy sexual abuse actually involve adult women.(34)

One might be able to forgive individual Roman Catholic clergy if one chooses to subscribe to the theory that these men are suffering from a sickness and this disease warrants as much sympathy as disgust, but it is the failure of church leaders in situation after situation to deal promptly and properly with both victims and perpetrators that is much more despicable and much harder to forgive. In case after case, church leaders failed to protect the abused victims. Rather than confess errors of judgment and acknowledge the pain suffered by victims, church leaders fought back in rather vicious ways.

In many cases, church officials, heeding the advice of legal counsel, immediately severed relationships with the children and families that were claiming sexual abuse. They were worried that any indication of sympathy or compassion would be seen as an admission of guilt for which they would ultimately end up paying in a court of law. However, in many cases, parishioners and the general public saw this reluctance on the part of church officials as an example of their lack of commitment and resolve. In most cases, it was merely a problem of perception, but it served to cast the vast majority of innocent clergy in a bad light. In reality, of course, most priests were very sympathetic, understanding, and caring, and they wanted desperately to reach out to those abused.

In essence, the victims became their enemies. In some situations, they even took part in the casting of stones at the accusers. Catholic lawyers advised priests and bishops to deny responsibility, evade accountability, and shut up. One lawyer was quoted as telling a priest who wanted to console a victim that "every conversation you have with a victim will cost the church a million dollars."(35)

In some instances, church leaders refused to hand over abusers' personnel records, protecting their priests as they callously turned their backs on the desperate pleas of children and other victims. In some cases, diocesan officials were encouraged to send files on priests who had been accused of sexual misdeeds to the Vatican embassy, where diplomatic immunity would protect documents from being subpoenaed.

In essence, the Roman Catholic Church responded to what they perceived to be a siege by an outside enemy by developing a siege mentality more consistent with large wealthy corporations that come under attack than a religious institution whose main products are love, compassion, caring, and sharing. Like a threatened Fortune 500 monolith, the church fought back using any means necessary, often resulting in many scared, angered, and puzzled longtime Catholics who had put their utmost trust in the Church throughout their lives.

The rank and file in the Catholic Church did not understand how supposed moral men, who were viewed to be above suspicion, could turn their backs on the poor, abused, and downtrodden. They could not comprehend how these devoted priests could purposely evade answers and accountability and tell half-truths about men who had obviously molested little children.

Father Thomas Doyle, an outspoken critic of the church that he loves so much and an advisor to the lawyer representing Father Sylvestre's victims, has described Catholic bishops in North America affected with sexual scandals as being:

[U]nchristian, arrogant and just plain stupid! They totally mishandle sexual abuse cases and then they still parade around in their funny outfits and demand respect. They have the intellectual depth of a layer of shellac. The phrase 'smart bishop' is like 'military intelligence' ... it's an oxymoron!(36)

Another disturbing aspect of the Roman Catholic Church's response to sexual abuse within its ranks is the fact that canon law is often given priority over secular criminal law.

This perversion of the course of justice is a criminal act. Documented cases reveal that church officials failed to report incidents to civil authorities, took deliberate steps to conceal evidence, and offered secret payouts to victims of child abuse. These and the efforts exerted to pressure victims and their families and independent witnesses into not reporting the incidents to the police tend to make some church officials appear less like the servants of Christ and more like Mafia crime bosses.

While incidents of child sexual abuse occurred with increasingly regularity throughout North America, in the Diocese of London nestled within the confines of balmy southwestern Ontario, all seemed innocent and almost idyllic. There was the Swales case in the early 1970s, but that was in the big city of London. Out in the honest hinterlands of Catholicism, evil and perverted things like that never happened

There were a few reports of incidents involving a Father Sylvestre in Windsor in 1954 and in Sarnia in 1962, but neither church officials nor the police who investigated each report could find any validity to the allegations. Official investigations decided it was not very serious, and no charges were filed.

In fact, Chatham-Kent Crown Attorney Paul Bailey believes that victims contacted police at least three times. Thrice, Father Sylvestre was accused. Thrice, church officials and the police ignored the victims' pleas. One might hypothesize there was almost something biblical about the whole thing.

In Chatham, Lou Ann Earle (Soontiens) was trying to make the best of a terrible childhood that was sadly lacking in love and parental care. She was looking forward, more so than many others her age, to attending St. Ursula's School. There, she speculated the understanding nature of the teachers, nuns, and possibly even the priest would offer her guidance, direction, protection, and hope for a brighter future.

Endnotes

18) Frank Bruni and Elinor Burkett. A Gospel of Shame (New York: Harper Collins Publishers Inc., 2002) :203.

19) Anne Simpkinson, "Soul Betrayal". Beliefnet. Date of Electronic Publication: May 11, 2006. Date Accesssed July 23, 2007 <http://www.beliefnet.com/story 10199.htm>.

20) Frank Bruni and Elinor Burkett. A Gospel of Shame. : 136

21) Bruni and Burkett. A Gospel of Shame :157

22) Bruni and Burkett. A Gospel of Shame : 158

23) Bruni and Burkett. A Gospel of Shame : 208

24) Stephen J. Rosetti A Tragic Grace (Cleegville. MN The Liturgical Press, 1996) :25.

25) Canadian Press, The Kelowna Spectator, December 2, 1992. : 6

26) Barbara McLintock, "Finally He Confesses". The Province. Date of Electronic Publication :June 16, 1998. Date Accessed: Julky 24, 2007. <http://sisis.nativeweb.org/reschool/jun1898bcri.htm>.

27) Stephen J. Rosetti. The Catholic Church and Child Sexual Abuse. America, The National Catholic Weekly Magazine. Date of Electronic Publication: April 22, 2002. Date Accessed: February 11, 2007 <http://www.catholicbookclub.net.htm>.

28) Jeffrey Weiss and Brooks Egerton, "Dallas Bishop To Offer Resignation" WFAA. Date of Electronic Publication: July 14, 2006 Date Accessed: May 5, 2007
< http://www.wfaa.com/sharedcontent/dws/wfaa/latestnewsstories f5343cc. html/.>

29) Barry Coldrey, "Religious Life Without Integrity" BishopAccountability.org. Date of Electronic Publication: April 10, 2000 Date Accessed: June 3, 2007 <http://bishopaccountability.org/reports2000_coldrey Integrity/integrity_03.htm.>

30) Sylvia McEachen , "Action On Sexual Abusive Parents Comes Only After Media Exposure". Lifestyle.net. Date of Electronic Publication: August 12, 2002 Date Accessed: June 6, 2007.

31) Helen Hull McClintock, "Independent Priest Canonist Is Abuser of Member of Bishop Review Board". Adoremus Bulletin Online Edition. Date of Electronic Publication: September 02, 2002 Date Accessed June 5, 2007. <http://adoremus.org/0902huels.htm.>.

32) Dr. J. Dominguez, How Many Catholic Priests Convicted". Clergy Sexual Abuse Scandals. Date of Electronic Publication: August 2003 Date Accessed: July 23,2007
<http://bibila.com/christianity/clergy.htm>.

33) Dr. J. Dominguez, "How Many Catholic Priests…"

34) Frank Bruni and Elinor Burkett. A Gospel of Shame (New York: Harper Collins Publishers Inc., 2002) :173

35) Frank Bruni and Elinor Burkett. A Gospel of Shame : 249.

36) Frank Bruni and Elinor Burkett. A Gospel of Shame :251.

Chapter Four

Lou Ann's Story

If there's really a God, would he have let this happen to a little girl like me?
Lou Ann Soontiens

When I first sat down with Lou Ann to hear her story, I had no idea what I would hear or how I would react. I suppose I must have had some vague expectations as to what her story would entail, along with many of the other women molested by Father Sylvestre had recounted in local, national, and even international media releases. But I was unprepared for her graphic and heart-wrenching approach that she took in recounting all of the indignities that she had endured for so much of her young life.

Lou Ann looked directly at me and told her story in a cool, calm, and direct manner. As time passed and her tale took shape, I was immediately struck by the fact that others must hear this story. They must hear it as I heard it. They must not hear it through my filtered interpretation, but hear it from Lou Ann herself. What follows is her story, told in her own honest, direct, and uncompromising manner.

***

I thought Father Sylvestre was my friend. He always made a point of telling me that I was special. That was important to me, for I had not felt that I was very special at all for most of my life. He seemed to sense my needs and always seemed to know what to say to cheer me up and give me confidence, a confidence that had sadly eluded me for much of my life.

My mother had abandoned me when I was only six weeks old. I never knew my father. In fact, I am not entirely sure if my mother really knew who my father was. If she did, she has never shared the information with me. Consequently, my maternal grandmother and step-grandfather raised me.

I looked forward to going to school each day. I especially felt Father Sylvestre was attempting to listen to me. As a result, I confided in him about almost everything. When I was in grade five, Father Sylvestre would regularly request that I come to the church and help him with a number of small tasks, like counting collection money, folding church bulletins, making banners, and so forth.

I initially felt honored. I was sure that he saw me as someone special. I was sure he could look into my soul and see who I really was. I was sure he could see a bright light shining there that would someday reveal itself to the rest of the world. When I was around him, I felt that my future was full of hope and promise and I had potential. Then everything changed.

The first time Father Sylvestre touched me, he put his hands over my breasts and fondled them. He then took his hands, inched them into my pants, and touched me below the waist. I barely moved, and I could not utter a word. I was confused and scared and in a state of absolute shock.

Why was Father doing this to me? What had I done to cause him to do this to me? It must have been something that I said or did. What other reason would he have for doing such things to me? After all, he was my friend. I trusted him. Was he not God's representative on earth?

After this initial experience, I ran home, seeking some sort of reassurance or possibly even an explanation. My words tumbled out of me in a jumble of phrases and questions that betrayed my hurt, fear, pain, and absolute confusion.

Angered and perhaps full of confusion as well, my grandfather reacted in a fashion that I would have expected if I had been a bit older. He ordered me to take a shower, as if water and soap could somehow wash away my wild, impertinent, and fantastic stories. I came out of the shower, dripping wet and even more frightened. My grandfather directed me to sit naked in a hard, cold wooden chair until he returned from discussing the matter with Father Sylvestre. I sat there full of trepidation and attempted to speculate what my grandfather would be saying to Father.

Would my grandfather be full of unmitigated anger with the priest? Would he stop this man from man doing such strange things to me? Would he bring this man, who I had so recently trusted, completely to task? For once in his life, would he come to the aid of his granddaughter?

I did not have long to wait for my answer to these questions. My grandfather returned home and confronted his naked, shaking granddaughter full of anger, but his ire was not directed at Father Sylvestre. Rather, it was at me. According to my grandfather, I was an ungrateful liar who only wanted to make trouble for a man of God who only wished to help me out and give me guidance in becoming a good Catholic girl.

I was instructed to get dressed. My grandfather took me back to the church, where I was forced to confess my sins to the good Father. In the privacy of the confessional, Father Sylvestre looked at me solemnly and said, "What I am doing to you is good, not bad, but you must not tell anyone. What is going on between us will be our special secret."

He once again played on my innocence, insecurities, and desperate need for love and attention by any adult who would play even the most superficial role as a loving parent. He told me, "Lou Ann, you are a special person to me, and I would never do anything to hurt you. Anything that I do for you, or to you, is for your own good. Because you are so young, you do not yet know what is good for you, but I do. So trust me."

Father Sylvestre would come to my class at school and request I be allowed to leave class to help him. I would be expected to visit him after school as well as on Sundays. I would stay after mass. My grandfather would pick me up when Father Sylvestre was satisfied that I had completed the tasks that he had assigned to me.

One time when he came to my classroom to recruit me for another supposed job, I balked and told my teacher, a nun, that I did not want to go.

"Father Sylvestre hurts me," I said.

The teacher dismissed my comments with a wave of her hand. She said, "You are a troubled child, and you must do as you're told. Now hurry up."

It was soon apparent that there was no point in seeking out allies or getting someone to listen to me. Not even teachers would place any credence in my protests. I was in a familiar position, alone, insecure, and with few viable options. No one would believe that Father Sylvestre, this seemingly kindly and affable man, was abusing me. For most people, it was simply unthinkable. Any protest on my part only served to make me appear difficult and alienated me from others even more.

My visits with Father Sylvestre would happen two, three, and sometimes even more times a week. The initial touching of my breasts and private parts had become practically every sexual act imaginable and more. Father Sylvestre would ejaculate all over my body—on my back, in my mouth, on my face, on my chest, and sometimes actually in my vagina. At other times, he would take objects such as a broom handle and forcibly put them into my vagina and anus.

I knew nothing about sexual matters, as I had no instruction in any aspect of this part of life. I simply knew that what Father Sylvestre was doing to me was instinctively wrong. I also knew that most of the things he did resulted in physical pain. The emotional and psychological pain came later.

When his abuse became painful and I started to bleed, I would ask him and sometimes beg him to stop. His response was not to cease his actions. Instead, he reprimanded and admonished me.

"Only good girls go to heaven, so you should always do whatever Father asks you to do."

When he was not abusing me, he could be very kind. He would often put his arm around me in a nonsexual fashion and tell me that he cared for me a great deal. In fact, he would sometimes tell me that he loved me.

I was caught in a horrible predicament. Father Sylvestre abused me and often caused me great physical pain, but at least he showed me some attention. It was attention and recognition that I sorely lacked within my own familial situation. Later, I realized that many sexual predators innately sense this kind of weakness, and they are quick to pounce upon their victims using every psychological trick in the book. I was a lamb being led to the slaughter by a sly and highly manipulative fox.

Soon he was having intercourse with me regularly. On one occasion, I returned to my grandparents' house, bleeding. Embarrassed and more than a little worried, I placed my bloodstained underwear in the laundry basket.

Over time, I began to hate myself for what was being done to me. I saw myself as ugly, and I grew to despise my body. Because I did not like myself, it was difficult to get others to care for me. I lacked real friends. I preferred to be alone. It is a characteristic that has plagued me all of my life. To this very day, I am a loner.

After a time, I began to assume a detached personality when Father Sylvestre was using and abusing me. I would emotionally, if not physically, escape from his grasp by having an out-of-body experience. In my mind's eye, I would escape to a safe spot where there was peace, beauty, and love. It was a safe haven free of pain and devoid of suffering. I would only return to the real world when he had finished with me.

When I returned home after another one of these abusive sessions, I would try to wash away the shame I felt. I would linger in my bath for as long as I could, constantly washing myself. I was Lady Macbeth, constantly scrubbing away that which could not be erased.

At first, I assumed I was alone in this abusive situation. Then I began to hear whisperings on the playground. The taunts would be directed toward an unhearing Father Sylvestre when he would be making his seemingly innocent regular visits to the school playground. The hushed voices that grew louder as time progressed spoke of "Father Feeler" and "Sylvestre the Molester." It began to dawn on me that I was mistaken and I was not alone. It was of little value. But, for someone who had spent the better part of her life alone, it offered a bit of solace.

I often wondered why those teachers, some of them nuns, did not hear those epithets being tossed in the direction of Father Sylvestre. Did they never stop and wonder, even if it were just in passing, why this holy man, this representative of God himself, was being described in such terms?

They must have heard those taunts because they grew louder as time passed. They were essentially the sound of a slightly more than quiet rebellion and protest. They may not have even known or could, if questioned, accurately vocalize their anger, but it was there nevertheless. The innocent souls on that playground knew in their heart of hearts that this man was not good nor was he associated with the God they had been told about. They knew innately that something was wrong with this man. They sensed there was evilness about him and he should be stopped.

I now think they wanted an adult to come to the rescue. They wanted a teacher, parent, or some adult to right the wrong they sensed was occurring. But no knight in shining armor was coming to the rescue. If the teachers on that playground heard, they did nothing, so my abuse, as well as that of many others, continued unabated.

As grade eight at St. Ursula's ended, I looked forward to my first year at "The Pines" (Ursuline College). I would be in high school, and I would no longer be attending a school in such close proximity to Father. But it proved to be only wishful thinking. Father Sylvestre was far from being done with me.

To simply enter the doors of secondary school, I needed to have Father's signature. When I went to see him, the same old things happened. It did not seem to matter to him that I was now graduating from elementary school and becoming more mature. Getting the signature required me to submit once again to the usual litany of sexual abuse. I was forced to perform oral sex on him and endure the usual fingering of various parts of my body. Only after he was fully satisfied did he agree to sign my papers. I, as before, left the rectory and went directly home to take a long bath and fantasize about how high school would be so much better than elementary school in all ways.

Unfortunately, it was to be only a fantasy. Father Sylvestre refused to relinquish his claim upon me. When I would return home from my classes in grade nine, my grandfather would be waiting there with instructions for me to attend upon Father Sylvestre, for he had some jobs for me to do and he needed my help. Some of these jobs included Father Sylvestyre taking graphic photographs of me in various poses and situations and involving me in a number of sexual acts.

When I was seventeen and after approximately five years of sexual abuse at the hands of Father Sylvestre, I began to feel ill almost daily. I was taken to the doctor, where he diagnosed me as pregnant. At that young age, I had not been with any other man in a sexual way other than Father Sylvestre. Being naïve and having no instruction from my grandparents about sex, I did not fully comprehend why I was pregnant, but I sensed it had something to do with what Father Sylvestre had been doing to me for so long.

Ever the good Catholic, my grandfather conferred with Father Sylvestre, as well as our family doctor, about what should be done about my situation. It was decided, unbeknownst to me and without my consent, that I was to have an abortion. The procedure could probably be best described as a back-alley abortion.

The result was severe hemorrhaging. I put a blood-soaked towel between my legs. I was so weak that I was barely conscious. I was taken to Victoria Hospital in London. There, on February 21, 1973, I underwent further surgery that hospital officials described as a "follow-up procedure to an incomplete abortion."

I was then sent home to a hospital in Chatham, where I spent another week before I was allowed to return home. I was now alone with my grandfather. My grandmother had died. The relationship with my grandfather, although assuming the form I wanted it to become, became even more complicated by my pregnancy. But it did not prepare me for one strange and disturbing incident that occurred between my grandfather and me.

On many a dark and lonely night, I have thought back to what my grandfather did one night after I had returned home from the hospital. After I had gone to bed, my grandfather thought I was asleep. He silently slipped into my room and sat on the bed beside me. I soon awoke and found him gently rubbing my stomach. Confused, frightened, and imagining the worst, I feared he was preparing to abuse me in the same manner that Father Sylvestre had been doing for so long. In retrospect, I have a different opinion of what my grandfather was really doing that night.

I wished I could have seen his face in the dim light of my bedroom that night. If I had, I sometimes wonder if I would have seen tears and a look of pained anguish upon his face. Had he, instead of seeking advice from Father Sylvestre, actually confronted him? Had he actually come to my defense for once in his life? Had he threatened Father?

I wish I knew. I would like to think that my grandfather finally realized I had been telling the truth. I want to believe that he finally realized that I was not a bad girl and I was somebody worthy of his love and, most of all, worthy of the protection that one expects from his or her grandfather.

I like to think back to that night and imagine the best about my grandfather. I like to think that he had an epiphany that night and he felt, even if it was just briefly, some of my pain that night. I like to think he was empathizing, in his own fashion, with what I had just recently undergone. Of course, I will never know for sure, but it doesn't stop me from wondering and hoping.

After living for approximately a week after my abortion with my grandfather, I decided I had to leave this home that never was, in any sense of the word, my home. I left his home with absolutely nothing. I was not allowed to take anything.

My grandfather so succinctly stated, "You came here with nothing, and you will leave here with nothing."

I never spoke with my grandfather again after that night. There was never any verbal acknowledgement of my abuse, nor would there be any apology from him. He died several years ago. Whatever he knew, suspected, thought, or felt went to the grave with him.

I escaped to a friend's home. Although I was forced to live in a small room in the basement, I felt for the first time in my life that I had some control over my life and actually had a bit of hope for the future.

I no longer had any contact with Father Sylvestre, so he no longer abused me. The abuse ended after I had my abortion. I was also no longer forced to live under the dictatorial conditions that my grandparents had imposed upon me. I was free, or at least I thought I was. As my life proceeded, I soon realized that I would never be truly free. Father Sylvestre would always be with me. He would haunt my hopes and dreams. Throughout my life, I would constantly find him lurking in every nook and cranny of my existence.

I soon outgrew my friend's home and the restrictions that were imposed upon me. I didn't like the fact that boys were living in the same house. After all, I was free. I wanted to experience life to its fullest. I didn't really know what I wanted, but I knew I needed something. I couldn't verbalize it then, but I think I was looking for love. I was looking for someone to care about me. I was looking for someone to give me back my childhood, innocence, and self-respect. It would not be an easy task or search.

I left school with only a grade nine education. I took the first job I was offered. I worked as a waitress in a restaurant to support myself until I met my first husband. I was eighteen years old when I married, but, in reality, I had the maturity of a twelve-year-old. I don't think I really knew what I was getting into. Other girls my age were getting married, so I felt I should do so as well. It seemed to make other girls happy. Maybe it would make me truly happy for the first time in my life. It did not.

The marriage resulted in two children being born very close together. As it turned out, I was not ready for such weighty responsibilities. I came to resent the fact that my husband seemed to be only interested in sex. The reality, of course, was that he had a normal sexual appetite. I, for reasons I could not share with him, did not.

Lacking a healthy intimate relationship, our marriage was doomed to fail. We kept it together for six years, but it should have ended much sooner. Before I knew it, I was a single mother living alone with two young children.

This had been the case throughout my life. I was caught between the devil and the deep blue sea. I was not happy being alone with two children, but I knew I was not yet ready to enter into a meaningful relationship with a man. But I was alone. Although I knew in my heart of hearts that I was not ready to seek that which I knew would elude me once again, I felt compelled to try it nevertheless. It was, as one might have speculated, another unhappy union.

My second husband was not always a loving man. He was typically abusive. Lacking in anything resembling self-confidence, I secretly pondered if I had somehow subconsciously sought out someone who would abuse me. After all, that was the first type of relationship that I had experienced. In some bizarre, psychologically messed-up manner, maybe that's the only thing that I really understood. Before the marriage could disintegrate any further, my second husband took ill and passed away.

Throughout these marriages, children, and just the normal stresses of living a life, I had to always endure my terrible "dirty little secret," as I always described it to myself. The abuse of my childhood never really let go of me. It possesses me in way or another at all times and generally has made my life, to a greater or lesser extent, a living hell.

Every day, I must live with the abuse that a priest inflicted upon an innocent child who put all of her trust in a man that society told was to be trusted. The brutal betrayal of that trust at such an early age has made me suspicious of everyone.

I wish I could trust so many people, but I can never take that final blind leap of faith that signifies true trust. I always feel in the back of my mind that, no matter who it is or how often he has demonstrated his loyalty and pledged his friendship, I can never allow myself to trust anyone completely and without the haunting hint of reservation.

I have tried all of my life to dismantle those walls, but I am unable to do so. The pain and hurt remains when all else is gone. I do not handle criticism very well. I left so many jobs simply because I could not handle any type of criticism, even if it was only mild criticism and meant to be constructive. I simply lacked self-confidence, and I have been paranoid for much of my life.

I once worked at a job where there was an issue of workplace harassment. The worker in question was punished, but, to my way of thinking, this co-worker's punishment did not live up to the crime. I left this job shortly after this incident.

I eventually realized that the only way I would be happy working would be if I worked on my own. I established my own business working with animals. I was happier than I had ever been. I seemed to be able to trust the animals. They never seemed to betray me. Their love for me was real and genuine.

I am very lucky now as I feel my life is slowly coming together. I am married to a wonderful man who truly cares for me and loves me. Maybe that old saying about the third time being the charm is true. I only know that I could not have gotten through all that I have endured in the last few years without his support. He, more so than anyone else, has played a big role in establishing our home as a safe haven for me. I need a place to escape to and a place where I know I will be protected, loved, and supported. Without that, I am once again that little twelve-year-old girl running scared.

It is not always easy, but I try very hard, and he tries even harder. He puts up with a lot from me. My desire for sexual intimacy is low. Although I try to reassure him that is not him but me, I am not always sure that he really understands. In reality, the truth of the matter is that it is neither my fault nor his, but that of a man of the cloth who I met before I even became a teenager.

One of the hardest things I ever had to do in my life was to tell my present husband about the abuse I had endured. He had been reading about the sexual abuse inflicted upon these other girls in the newspaper. His immediate reaction was to defend Father Sylvestre and say something like, "Look what these terrible women are doing to poor Father Sylvestre."

At first, I made no comment. I had kept this horrible secret all my life, so why would I want to bear the consequences of revealing it now? I was worried that it might harm our marriage, and I was horribly unsure of how my husband would react to my stories of abuse. However, I also realized that it was time to tell my story. If other women were coming forward, why wouldn't I do the same thing? I was tired and fed up with having to keep such a long-standing and psychologically damaging secret. If I wanted to have a truly honest and open relationship with the man I loved, I would have to tell him the complete truth.

When I first revealed my story to my husband, he never once expressed disbelief. He immediately offered genuine support. Over time, he gradually realized that priests are not saints, but merely humans who, like the rest of us, can be good or bad. They can have illnesses and perversions like anyone else in society. The real crime, as he soon realized, were the lies, cover-up, and lack of real care for the victims expressed by the Catholic Church as a whole.

My children are also wonderfully supportive and understanding. I try every day to be the kind of mother that I wished so many times that I had been able to have. I always fear that I will, because of my abuse, turn into a horrible mother. I am not always the easiest person to live with on a daily basis. I have a short fuse, and I can be very irritable with others. That has occasionally included my children.

On some days, as there have been throughout my life, I feel terribly vulnerable, discouraged, and depressed. I sometimes withdraw into myself. On more than one occasion, I have felt that I am worthless and my entire life has been a personal failure. I must constantly fight against those feelings. Although my therapy sessions have certainly helped me, there are days when waves of sadness overcome me and I wonder just exactly who I am.

No matter how much I try and how many ways I have attempted to rationalize my situation and the things that happened to me so long ago, I cannot get past certain feelings. I have lost my faith in God, and I know I will never retrieve it. I hear the cries of my inner voice silently screaming in frustration and anger. "God could have stopped this. God could have stopped the abuse and helped me, and he didn't."

I feel betrayed by Father Sylvestre, but I also feel more betrayed by God and the Catholic Church. It was their fault that I had to leave school early, I trust no one, I live in fear, and my entire life has been destroyed. I have trouble simply walking down into the basement of my own house because it reminds me too much of the basement at the rectory where I was abused.

I sometimes have the most vivid nightmares that Father Sylvestre is coming after me and he wants to kill me. He has already killed a good part of me. In my dreams, I see him trying to inflict the final blow.

Will it ever end? I sometimes think I will always be that frightened, wet, naked, twelve-year-old girl sitting on a cold kitchen chair, waiting for my grandfather to come home after talking to Father Sylvestre and being forced to confess my sins to the transgressor.

Forgive you, Father, for it is you that has sinned.

LOU ANN EARLE – GRADE 5

It was during her days of an elementary student at St. Ursula's School in Chatham, Ontario that Lou Ann's sexual abuse at the hands of Father Sylvestre commenced. It began with her being asked to come to the rectory and help out with small church-related tasks that quickly evolved into inappropriate touching (Courtesy of Lou Ann Soontiens).

LOU ANN EARLE – GRADE 7-8

As the end of her elementary school life drew to a close, Lou Ann was looking forward to attending secondary school across town at Ursuline College and escaping from the unwanted attentions of Sylvestre. By this time, she was experiencing even greater abuses at the hands of Father Sylvestre.(Courtesy of Lou Ann Soontiens)

LOU ANN EARLE – GRADE 9-10

When Lou Ann left St. Ursula's School, she soon found out that secondary school was not to provide a refuge for her from Father Sylvestre. When she would arrive home from high school, her grandfather would often advise her that Father Sylvestre had requested her presence at the rectory in order to "do a few jobs". She became pregnant with Sylvestre's child in grade 10 and had an abortion at the hospital in London, ON in February of 1973. (Courtesy of Lou Ann Soontiens)

LOU ANN SOONTIENS – 2007

Failed marriages, bouts of depression, lost jobs and feelings of worthlessness haunted Lou Ann for a good portion of her life. It was not until 2005, when Sylvestre was arrested and charged, that Lou Ann was able to begin the healing process and discuss that which she had kept secret for so many years.
(Courtesy of Chatham Daily News)

Jim Gilbert

PICTURE OF ST. JOACHIM ROAD SIGN

Charles Sylvestre was born on September 2, 1922 in the small, predominantly French Canadian village of St. Joachim, situated in Essex County. He was to live here with his parents until he left to attend school in Sudbury in 1936. (Author's collection)

CHURCH AT ST. JOACHIM

It was at this church (now closed) that Sylvestre was baptized by his uncle, who was a priest, the day following his birth. He attended this church along with his parents for most of his early days. Like many other Catholic families of the time, there was a great deal of pride in the fact that Charles chose to enter the priesthood.
(Author's Collection)

ST. ALPHONSUS CHURCH, WINDSOR

After being ordained as a priest from St. Peter's Seminary in London on May 21st, 1948, Father Sylvestre was made associate pastor at St. Alphonsus Church in Windsor, Ontario. (Author's Collection)

MOUNT ST. JOSEPH , LONDON

After reportedly abusing four girls while associate pastor at Sacred Heart Parish in Windsor,(1954-1956), Sylvestre was given the position of bursar at King's College in London as well as chaplain at Mount St. Joseph's girls' school. While chaplain here, two girls are reportedly abused by Sylvestre. (Author's Collection)

Breach of Faith, Breach of Trust

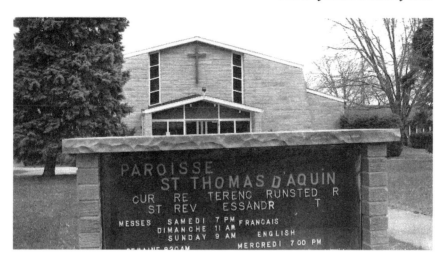

ST. THOMAS AQUINAS, SARNIA

During the years 1958-1962, Father Sylvestre was posted to this church in Sarnia. During his time as pastor at this church he reportedly abused at least seven girls at the school (St. Thomas Aquinas School) associated with this church. It was also during his stay at this church that Sylvestre's abuse was reported to the Sarnia police. (Author's Collection)

ST. URSULA'S CHURCH – FRAME STRUCTURE

From 1968-1980, Father Sylvestre was assigned to St. Ursula's Church in Chatham. and during that time he was accused of molesting at least twenty nine women. Lou Ann Soontiens attended mass at the original St. Ursula's Church, which was removed in 1977 from the present day church site, to the Bothwell area where it became part of a a youth camp as is pictured here. (Author's Collection)

ST. URSULA'S CHURCH 1978 - PRESENT DAY

On approximately the same site as the original frame church, a new brick church was built in the late 1970s. Father Sylvestre was the pastor at the new church as well as the old one and it was in the rectory of the new church that many of the younger twenty-nine victims were molested. (Author's Collection)

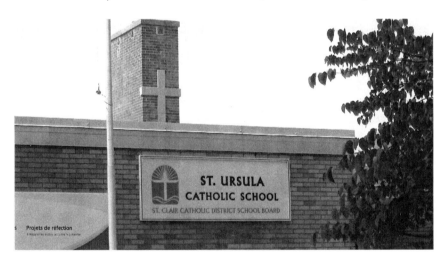

ST. URSULA'S SCHOOL – PRESENT DAY

All twenty-nine victims of Father Sylvestre attended this school between 1968 and 1980. Sylvestre would arrange to get many of the victims that he abused to be excused from classes in order to "help him with church chores". Once at the rectory, he would often fondle students while other students were present (Author's Collection)

ST. URSULA'S SCHOOL – PRESENT DAY

All twenty-nine victims of Father Sylvestre attended this school between 1968 and 1980. Sylvestre would arrange to get many of the victims that he abused to be excused from classes in order to "help him with church chores". Once at the rectory, he would often fondle students while other students were present (Author's Collection)

FATHER SYLVESTRE COURT APPEARANCE

On July 21st, 2005 Chatham-Kent Police arrested Sylvestre at his home in Belle River and charged him with three counts of indecent assault, one of rape and one of sexual intercourse with a female under fourteen years of age. Sylvestre is pictured here leaving the Chatham Kent Courthouse after one of his appearances in September 2006. (Courtesy of Chatham Daily News)

CHIEF CARL HERDER AND DETECTIVE CONSTABLE KATE McCARTHUR

Inspector George Flickwert and Detective Constable Kate McCarthur of the Chatham Kent Municipal Police Department garnered a great deal of praise, respect as well as awards for not only the way they handled the entire Father Sylvestre case but also for their sensitive approach to the victims involved.
(Courtesy of Chatham Daily News)

CHATHAM KENT CROWN ATTORNEY – PAUL BAILEY

Crown Attorney Paul Bailey took a personal interest in the prosecution of Father Charles Sylvestre and was a tireless advocate for the forty three victims. He was a strong critic of the inadequate manner in which the Catholic Church handled its offending priests. (Courtesy Chatham Daily News)

LONDON DIOCESE SELLING BISHOP'S RESIDENCE

In February of 2007 the London Diocese reported that they would be selling the bishop's residence in London (pictured here) as well other properties in order "to help pay for sexual abuse claims". (Author's Collection)

FATHER SYLVESTRE DIES IN JAIL

On January 22, 2007 Father Charles Sylvestre died, after serving less than four months of his three year sentence, in a Kingston Penitentiary hospital. It is believed that his remains are buried in this family plot in St. Joachim alongside his mother and father.(Author's Collection)

LOU ANN SOONTIENS AWARDED 1.75 MILLION DOLLARS

After years of abuse and difficult negotiations with the London Diocese, Soontiens was awarded almost two million dollars on May 8, 2009. She is shown here during the long awaited press conference announcing the largest settlement in Canadian history for an individual sexual abuse victim. In the background a picture of her younger self looks on. (Courtesy of Chatham Daily News)

Chapter Five

God or Someone Could Have or Should Have Stopped Him

As tragic as what has happened to victims, it also tragic for parishioners when priests who have faithfully served their people, turn out to men with a dark compulsive and predatory sides.
Henry Flynn, *Sexual Abuse in the Catholic Church (2003)*

Lou Ann, the other forty-six victims, and perhaps many more who have never come forward are very justified in not only wondering why God allowed this abuse to happen to young innocents, but why did God's representatives on earth allow it to happen? It was certainly not because it had never happened before.

Earlier, I outlined a few of the many cases that have occurred involving sexual abuse among Catholic clergy since the fifth century throughout the world. However, some even more recent cases happened in North America that mirrored Father Sylvestre's actions to an almost eerie degree.

In April 2002, Lori Haigh, a thirty-seven-year-old woman from the Dioceses of Orange and Los Angeles, alleged in a lawsuit that she had been abused from the age of fourteen to seventeen by Father John Lenihan. Lori alleged the abuse took place some twenty years before and had resulted in her becoming pregnant and having an abortion, which the priest paid for. She stated the priest had regularly molested her on numerous occasions. He had easy access to her, as she was involved in church activities five days a week. "Father John," as he was known during his tenure at St. Norbert Church, would abuse her in the church, in the rectory, and even in his car at secluded spots.(37)

When she went to complain about this abuse to other priests in 1982, one priest made sexual advances toward her. Another accused her of lying and told her that he "never wanted to see her in the church again."(38)

In 2002, Father Lenihan admitted to a number of incidents involving sexual improprieties and agreed to be removed from the priesthood. Shortly afterwards, Lori received a settlement of $1.2 million. When asked why she had not come forward before, she responded that, because of her previous experience with unsympathetic Catholic priests, "it would have been futile."(39)

While the students at St. Ursula's School in Chatham, Ontario, warned others on the playground that "Father Feeler" or "Sylvestre the Molester" was in the vicinity, the students at St. Mary's Grammar School in Fall River, Massachusetts, had their own warning system. When they saw Father James Porter in the halls of their school, the warning "Father Porter's coming! Father Porter's coming!" echoed from corridor to corridor. The girls in their bobby socks and knee-length skirts pressed their backs against the hard walls in order to avoid the priest coming up behind them and getting his hand underneath their skirts.(40)

Boys at the Fall River Grammar School were not exempt from Father Porter's unwanted attention either. He would grab at the crotches of the young boys and give them slobbery French kisses on their birthdays. Oftentimes, these open and inappropriate displays of affection were done in front of the nuns teaching at the school, who remained silent and arguably in a state of shock.(41)

Lou Ann and other victims of Father Sylvestre wondered, as did the students in Fall River, why the nuns and teachers at the school did not know about their plights, why they did not come to their aid, or why they did not say something to these priests.

In both situations, the sisters probably remained silent for a variety of reasons. Many might have had no idea that anything untoward was going on at all. Others refused to believe that God's representative on earth would do anything that would harm a child. For others, it was simply beyond their very basic and naïve understanding of sexual matters. They would not have been able to accurately voice what they could not even imagine was going on. Some other nuns may simply have been too frightened to accuse their superiors (the priests) of such heinous crimes. Underlying all of these reasons may have been the distinct possibility that, if any nun had accused a priest of such crimes, she may have been subjected to disbelief, ridicule, and censure.

No matter what the many reasons were, the nuns at St. Ursula's in Chatham, Ontario; St. Mary's in Fall River, Massachusetts; and hundreds of other Catholic schools remained silent bystanders and unknowing witnesses to the sexual abuse by the revered men in black whom they trusted and respected with absolute faith.

As in the Father Sylvestre situation, the fact that other priests and nuns seemed to ignore what was going on, the students at St. Mary's and St. Ursula's felt that it must, in some manner, unknown in their limited experiences, be acceptable. Most of the students in both Ontario and Massachusetts decided to keep quiet and suffer the consequences.

It is interesting to note that, in both Father Porter's and Father Sylvestre's case (as well as many others), the students began to blame themselves. They somehow felt they had done something to make their respected and often-loved priests to do these things to them. One student from St Mary's so succinctly stated, "How can you tell your parents that God did this to you?"(42)

The silent pain continued in Father Porter's situation until September 1990. A former St. Mary's student, Frank Fitzpatrick, like Lou Ann and many other victims of Father Sylvestre, was often so depressed, unhappy, and moody that he decided to do something about it. Fitzpatrick began a one-man campaign to track down Father Porter and attempt to find other abused students and ultimately bring Porter to justice. After a number of dead ends, reluctant witnesses, and numerous disappointments, Father Porter was brought to trial in June 1992 to face abuse charges against fifty-four victims.

Victims of Father Porter poured out their stories, as did the victims of Father Sylvestre, in floods of repressed emotion and anger. They spoke of suffering the unwanted attentions of the Massachusetts priest in quiet school corridors, playgrounds, the churchyard, the sacristy, the town pool, the beach, church camp, the green around the statue of the Virgin Mary, and even the altar.(43)

Abused victims of Porter also told stories of the impact upon their emotional, sexual, and psychological well-being in later years. Their stories bore uncanny similarities to those told by Lou Ann and other victims of Father Sylvestre. The Porter victims spoke of broken marriages, alcoholism, drug abuse, suicide attempts, nervousness in crowds, fears of intimacy, sexual confusion, lifelong depression, and prolonged therapy sessions. As in the Sylvestre case, the sheer number of complaints and vivid graphic abuse descriptions by so many victims gradually served to bring home the fact that Father Porter had brought tremendous devastation to dozens, if not hundreds, of young, innocent victims.

As in southwestern Ontario, once the victims' stories started pouring out, the obvious questions started to be asked. How many children had been molested? For how long? In how many parishes? How long had church officials known about this?

In Father Porter's situation, church officials received their first complaint about Porter even before he was ordained. He had been moved, like Father Sylvestre, several times in his career in order to avoid scandal and in response to complaints. Like Father Sylvestre, church officials in Massachusetts never:

Barred Porter from contact with children
Called the police
Warned parents
Reached out to the victims in a meaningful fashion
Tried to expel him from the priesthood

Father Sylvestre and Father Porter, if they had ever met, would have had much to talk about, but probably not nearly as much as both sets of their victims.

Why Did God Allow This to Happen?

Wondering why God allowed this to happen is a very understandable and common question that innocent victims in hundreds of unfair situations ask. In the case of sexual abuse within the Catholic Church, the question should be directed toward a much less mystical power.

Why did the Roman Catholic Church hierarchy allow the sexual abuse of Lou Ann and hundreds, if not thousands, of other victims to continue despite the fact that many priest molesters had been already identified? In order to adequately answer that question, a number of things must be considered.

Some critics have argued that the very job description for being a Catholic priest reads like an ad looking for pedophiles. One priestly scholar, in a slightly exaggerated, tongue-in-cheek manner, created the following fictional "Help Wanted" ad:

> Must be an unmarried young adult male, not interested in relationships with adult women yet not an acknowledged homosexual, love working with children especially in unsupervised situations like youth groups or altar servers and believe one has a special relationship with God such that one should be placed in a position of authority due to it.(44)

Until the Catholic Church carefully examines its recruitment policies in order to avoid men with the demographics and behavioral traits of pedophiles, nothing will really change. Simple statements by the Vatican, bishops, public relations firms hired by individual dioceses, and various well-intentioned religious councils cannot make them disappear, nor assure anyone that this type of behavior will no longer be tolerated.

Although the Roman Catholic Church would vehemently vow that they strictly adhere to the Bible's New Testament, it would appear they have some problems interpreting one particular statement attributed to Jesus when addressing his disciples. In Matt 18:6, Mark 9:42, and Luke 17:2, Jesus stated, "Whoever causes one of these little ones who believe in me to sin, it would be better for him if a great millstone were put around his neck and he were thrown into the sea." Despite their protestations, some specific church doctrines and traditional practices show a wide gap between beliefs and practice.

For example, the Catholic Church continues to adamantly advocate the concept that, as long as a priest is ordained, his personal transgressions have no effect on his ability and right to say mass, perform baptisms, give absolutions, and administer all the sacraments of the Church. The concept of "once a priest, always a priest" flies in the face of the very message delivered by Jesus. As long as an ordained priest continues to possess these almost superhuman powers, he will continue to be allowed into situations where sexual abuse can occur again. Sexual abuse within the Catholic Church continued unabated throughout North America during the last twenty years, partially because of the failure by senior church leaders to report crimes committed by their ordained priests to the authorities.

In fact, Cardinal Joseph Ratzinger, in his role as prefect for the Congregation for the Doctrine of Faith, sent a letter to all Catholic bishops in 2001 stating very clearly that "the Church's investigations into claims of child sex abuse" were subject to "the pontifical secret" and were "not to be reported to law enforcement agencies" until church investigations were

completed "on pain of excommunication." The fact that Cardinal Ratzinger is now Pope Benedict XVI creates a very real concern that the old ways of "shut up and lay low" will continue to be the official stance of the Vatican.(45)

If the Catholic Church ever hopes to eradicate sexual abuse within the institution, it must come to terms with the concept that it is not above the law. It must report to the proper authorities all suspected incidents of clergy abuse immediately. The days of subterfuge, concealment, or withholding evidence to protect the reputation of the Catholic Church must end.

In an ironic twist of fate, it has been the reluctance of the church to report these crimes that has damaged the church's reputation in a manner that some might consider to be irreparable. As far back as 1972, reputable psychological studies demonstrated the peculiar and somewhat disturbing profiles of Roman Catholic priests. Dr. Eugene Kennedy and respected Catholic scholar Victor Heckler completed a study that found that 74 percent of the priests in their study (218) had "not resolved psychosexual problems and issues usually worked through in adolescence." The report concluded that "sexuality is, in other words, non-integrated into the lives of underdeveloped priests and many of them function at a pre-adolescent or adolescent level of psychosexual growth."(46)

Although he was not part of this study, it is interesting to note that, according to reports, Father Sylvestre, in his own psychological analysis, was determined to have demonstrated obvious adolescent tendencies. In addition, therapists described Father John Geoghan, another clerical abuser, as being "like an eighteen-year-old with all the good and bad that entails."(47)

Kennedy and Heckler stated that many priests had a poor sense of personal identity and command of interpersonal relationships. Priests live with peculiar handicaps, under peculiar stresses, that might foster child sexual abuse. They are often so out of touch with their own sexuality that they do not even realize that they have sexual feelings. (48)

Many therapists speculate that priests who molest may not recognize what they are feeling sexually. They may not be watchful of the boundary between acceptable and unacceptable behavior or even realized when they have crossed it:

> They don't know their sexual insides and as a result do not know how to properly and safely handle their natural sexual desires. As a result it sometimes comes out inappropriate ways like sexual abuse and their sexual instinct becomes uncontrollable.(49)

Because most priests have never been taught to deal with their sexual urges and have not been provided with acceptable ways and means to satisfy these urges, the resultant actions can be disastrous. Many priests are, on many levels, children themselves. Their only feelings of courtship and romance date to their pre-teen or early teen years. As a result, they turn to someone whom they may see as a sexual peer. They feel more comfortable with a child or a teenager as "the young boy or girl probably represents sexual awakening or unfinished business."(50)

The power and control entrusted to Catholic priests also partially answer the question as to why and how priests have been able to molest individuals, like Lou Ann, with no sense of the repercussions involved. Many Catholics perceive priests as their conduits to God, men who walk with one foot on earth and one foot in heaven. Catholic children are often taught that the priest speaks the direct messages of God in the form of the Gospel from the altar during mass.

In the case of the Catholic Church and their priests, there is a deep-seated and firmly established aura of trust and complete confidence. This can be a dangerous situation within a church, where priests have traditionally been encouraged to interact with young children in a variety of situations. According to a Denver therapist, Gail Ryan, who specializes in sexual abuse counseling, "the higher the level of trust and authority, the more vulnerable a child will be."(51)

While the vast majority of priests have a healthy, safe, and positive relationship with children, the environment does exist for molesting priests to take advantage of this trust and use it to abuse virtually without impunity.

Unlike many other religions, the Catholic Church embraces and espouses the belief that it is the one and only true faith. It is a monopoly, one that does not always see itself as subject to any kind of public regulation. Bishops are lords of their individual dioceses. Many see themselves answerable only to the pope. This is a major problem, as it leads the church to react in a fashion that does not lend itself to a public and rapid response to the problem. Many bishops see no reason to report abuses to authorities outside of the church. Of course, the abuse may very well continue because of this attitude.

The very culture of a Catholic Church that encourages deference and obedience and inspires confidence and trust in all matters creates a dangerous culture that goes a long way to answer the how and why of sexual abuse within the church.

Sexual molestation among priests has continued virtually unabated in the last twenty years in North America and to various degrees throughout the entire history of the Catholic Church, largely because of the very nature of the church. As a result, it is only when the very nature of the Catholic Church changes that the threat of sexual abuse by the clergy within the church will abate. It is a systemic problem that cosmetic alterations will not and cannot solve. Psychotherapist and ex-priest Richard Snipe succinctly stated, "Someone has to tell the church leaders that, by the very nature and organization of the Catholic Church, they have booked passage on the sexual *Titanic*."(52)

Endnotes

37) William Lobdell, "John Lenihan, Priest Who Admitted To Sex Abuse of Teen Agrees To Leave The Clergy". SNAP. Date of Electronic Publication:March 29, 2002 Date Accessed: June 12, 2007 <http:www snapnetwork.org/news/calif/lenihan_leaves_clergy.htm>.

38) William Lobdell, "John Lenihan, Priest...".

39) William Lobdell, "John Lenihan, Priest...".

40) Frank Bruni and Elinor Burkett, A Gospel of Shame (New York: Harper Collins Publishers Inc., 2002) : 6.

41) Frank Bruni and Elinor Burkett, A Gospel of Shame : 7.

42) Frank Bruni and Elinor Burkett, A Gospel of Shame : 10.

43) Frank Bruni and Elinor Burkett, A Gospel of Shame : 8.

44) Marie Fortune and Merle W. Longwood, eds. Sexual Abuse In The Catholic Church (The Haworth Pastoral Press, 2003) : 36 -37.

45) James Doward, "Pope Obstructed Sex Abuse Inquiry". GuardianUnlimited. Date of Electronic Publication: April 24, 2005 Date Accessed ": May 26, 2007 <http://observer.guardian.co.uk/international/story/0,6903,1469055.htm>.

46) Eugene Kennedy and Victor Heckler, The Catholic Priest In The United States: Psycholgical Investigations (Washington, DC, U.S. Cathoilc Conference, 1972) : 42.

47) Eugene Kennedy and Victor Heckler, The Cathoilc Priest.... : 43.

48) Eugene Kennedy and Victor Heckler, The Catholic Priest... : 46

49) Eugene Kennedy and Victor Heckler, The Catholic Priest...: 52.

50) Frank Bruni and Elinor Burkett, A Gospel of Shame (New York: Harper Collins Publishers Inc.) : 54-55.

51) Frank Bruni and Elinor Burkett, A Gospel of Shame : 58-59.

52) Frank Bruni and Elinor Burkett, A Gospel of Shame : 62.

Chapter Six

Sylvestre the Molester

On the playground, when Father Sylvestre was walking around, some of the older students would say: "Here comes Sylvestre the Molester!" or "Here comes Father Feeler!" A lot of students seemed to know about him.
Lou Ann Soontiens

Very little on the surface of Charles Sylvestre's early life indicated he would someday be given such sinister monikers as "Sylvestre the Molester" and "Father Feeler" by grade eight students who were frightened, confused, and repulsed.

Spotted at St. Ursula's School, roaming the playground and stalking new victims or searching for old ones, the students who knew would spread the word in their own way. Beginning in whispered tones and becoming louder and louder as time went on, they would warn others that "Father Feeler's on the prowl" or "Here comes Sylvestre the Molester."(53) Partly in jest, partly in disgust, and with more than a little fear, the students were subconsciously attempting to get someone to acknowledge a monster in priest's robes was lurking in a place that they instinctively knew should be a safe haven.

He was born Charles Henri Sylvestre in St. Joachim, Ontario, on September 2, 1922, and baptized the very next day by his uncle, also a Catholic priest. Sylvestre attended primary school in St. Joachim in the mid-1930s and lived with his family on a local farm.(54) From 1944 to 1948, Sylvestre studied philosophy and theology at St. Peter's Seminary in London, Ontario. While he was at the seminary, the concept of how to live a celibate life was probably either ignored or glossed over. According to recent research:

> Seminary training throughout the Catholic Church is inadequate in the training of sexuality which then heightens the possibility of future sexual misconduct. (55)

As a result, one can credibly conclude that Sylvestre's own training at St. Peter's Seminary did not handle the whole concept of human sexuality very well and he was probably not prepared to face a priestly, celibate life in any meaningful manner.

After being ordained in May 1948 in London, he was assigned to his first position as an assistant pastor at St. Alphonsus Parish in Windsor, Ontario. He stayed at this parish until 1953 when he was transferred to Hamilton in order to establish the French-speaking parish of St. Charles Garnier. Once the parish was up and running, Sylvestre was assigned an associate pastor position at Sacred Heart Parish in Windsor, as well as at Sacred Heart Parish in La Salle, a suburb of Windsor.

While he was at these parishes, the first reports of his sexual abuse became public. Four girls from Sacred Heart School in Windsor were to later accuse Father Sylvestre of abusing them at this time. Although it is quite possible that he abused others before this time, it represents the first recorded incidence of his abuse.(56)

One of the girls who was abused at this time approached another priest at the Windsor parish and told him what Father Sylvestre had done to her. The priest assured the frightened and confused thirteen-year-old girl that everything would be okay and he would "take care of it." "Taking care of it" was code in the Catholic Church for moving the priest to another parish. That is exactly what happened to Father Sylvestre.

Soon after these initial reports of abuse in Windsor, Father Sylvestre was transferred to King's College in London, where he served as bursar as well as the chaplain at Mount St. Joseph's, an all-girl school. It is only logical to assume that Sylvestre was relieved of his responsibilities in Windsor, at the very least, due to alleged sexual abuse complaints. Taking this into consideration, his placement as chaplain at an all-girl school in London certainly makes one stop and wonder what the Catholic officials in the Diocese of London were thinking. Unsurprisingly, Sylvestre, before he left Mount St. Joseph, was suspected of abusing at least two other girls.(57)

From 1958 to 1962, Reverend Sylvestre was assigned a position at St. Thomas Aquinas Church in Sarnia, which had St. Thomas Aquinas School affiliated with it. During his tenure in Sarnia, he was later to be accused of molesting seven girls. Among those girls was Diane Gauthier.(58)

Diane spoke to her teacher at St. Thomas Aquinas School and tried to explain what Father Sylvestre had done to her. The young Diane expected an explanation, a promise to explore the matter, or at least a sympathetic ear. But what she received instead was a stern lecture and placement in a dark closet as a form of punishment for her outrageous allegations.(59) The punishment that Diane received is reminiscent of the type of treatment that Lou Ann received from her grandfather for her accusations involving Father Sylvestre.

In 1962, the sister and the cousin of one of the abused girls brought a complaint against Father Sylvestre to the attention of the Sarnia Police Department. The police in Sarnia apparently began an investigation into the reported abuse, but, when they went to St. Thomas Aquinas Parish to question Sylvestre, they were told he had been sent to Montreal. Apparently, the police dropped the investigation into the matter at this time.(60)

Diocesan records of the time (1963) seem to indicate that Sylvestre was put on a leave of absence and sent to Holy Cross Fathers in Montreal on a retreat. It was generally accepted that this facility in Montreal was designed for those priests who were attempting to recover from bouts of alcoholism. There is nothing on file to suggest he was also being treated for his sexually abusive nature.

In 2007, in response to the release of these records, Peter Lauwers, legal counsel for the Diocese of London, stated, "From the documentary record, it appears that some of his victims advised the police who carried out an investigation." Lauwers also stated, "These witness statements were given by the Sarnia police to Monsignor J.A. Cook in Sarnia." Monsignor Cook "appears to have put the documents into an old envelope that he had postmarked 1958" and "likely gave a copy directly to Bishop Cody" of the Diocese of London."(61)

There is also reason to believe that Sylvestre spent a brief period at St. Michael's College in Toronto enrolled in a course. According to reports, he was not doing well in the course and petitioned Bishop Cody and Diocese of London to move him back into a parish.

Apparently, his request was granted. After only one semester at St. Michael's, he was assigned to do various types of tasks at parishes in Delhi, Windsor, and Saint Ceilia Church in Port Dover. At the latter position, he later claimed he started to have bouts of heavy drinking. From 1963 to 1968, he was also working as a bursar and librarian at Regina Mundi Catholic College in London, Ontario.(62)

In 1968, Father Sylvestre was assigned to the position of pastor at St Ursula's Catholic Church in Chatham. He was to remain the longest here. Here, he also would molest at least twenty-nine young girls between the ages of seven and fourteen over the next twelve years. At St. Ursula's, Father Sylvestre would gain the dubious distinction of being one of the worst pedophile priests in Canadian history. In looking back at his time at St. Ursula's in Chatham, it could be assumed that Sylvestre developed a dedicated pattern of overwork, drinking, and acting out sexually with young girls, which was to continue for the remainder of his life as a priest.

Carol Ann Mieras, like Lou Ann, was a bright, innocent young girl when Father Sylvestre began to exert his unwanted attentions upon her. Carol Ann reported that Sylvestre repeatedly abused her and would often abuse her as well as another young victim at the same time. One of these sessions with a classmate took place in the church rectory on Palm Sunday. Mieras maintains that she reported the abuse to a teacher (a nun) at St. Ursula's School, but was ignored.

Adamant that someone listen to her plight, she approached the Chatham Police Department in 1989. A detective took her statement. According to the police records and the detective's recollections, an investigation of the abuse at the hands of Father Sylvestre was started, but, due to lack of evidence and corroborating stories from other credible witnesses, the matter was dropped. In a statement to the media, Carol Ann outlined that the police investigator told her that there was simply no good reason to continue the investigation and she should simply leave it alone.(63)

Carol Ann has wondered if the investigation was rather incomplete because the investigator was a member of St. Ursula's Parish. The detective in question has refused to talk to the media about his role in this matter, other than to say there was an investigation but there was not enough information to proceed any further. To this day, Carol Ann remains a bit skeptical.(64)

In 1989, Carol Ann wrote a letter to Bishop John Sherlock of the Diocese of London that outlined some of the abuse that she had to endure as a young girl at the hands of Sylvestre. The bishop responded to her letter and arranged to meet with her at St. Patrick's Church in London. When Carol Ann arrived at the church for the meeting, she was informed that the bishop would not be meeting with her, as he was too busy. He had arranged for her to meet with another priest who would listen to her story. The message to Carol Ann was loud and clear. The diocese did not take her story seriously. Like dozens of other priests, bishops, church officials, and police officers throughout North America had done in many other similar situations, the official dance of denial had begun.(65)

Carol Ann must have felt, among many other things, very alone and singled out, but the reality of the situation was that, in the late 1980s and early 1990s, hundreds of victims of sexual abuse at the hands of priests were having the same frustrating time convincing church and police officials to listen and act. Carol Ann didn't realize it then, but in a few years, she would have it made very clear to her that, not only was she one of hundreds in North America, she was one of between fifty and one hundred within her own diocese.

In 1980, Bishop Sherlock moved Sylvestre after he had spent more than a decade of virtually unabated sexual abuse of at least thirty young girls at St. Ursula's Church in Chatham to Immaculate Conception Parish in Pain Court, a small French-speaking village a few miles west of Chatham. During his time at this church (1980–1989), the Diocese of London documented that he had molested at least four girls.(66)

In 1989, the Diocese of London, as well as several other Catholic dioceses throughout North America, implemented a sexual abuser policy. One of the cornerstones of this policy states unequivocally that "all diocesan priests must report all instances of sexual impropriety to the diocese's sexual abuse committee" and "members of the priesthood are not to exercise any discretion in fulfilling this reporting obligation."(67)

When asked by the media in February 1989 about this new policy, Bishop Sherlock avowed he had not received complaints of any sexual abuse of children in his diocese. It was simply to prepare for the possibility of it happening at some future time. He fervently told the Toronto newspaper that he was insisting the Diocese of London "be as forthright and open as possible."(68)

In August 1989, three months after Sylvestre had been removed from Pain Court's Immaculate Conception Church, he was assigned the role of chaplain at Hotel Dieu Grace Hospital in Windsor. The head of this new sexual abuse committee, Father Richard Tremblay, met with Pain Court officials. Allegations of sexual abuse concerning at least one of the four girls he had molested was investigated. A report was even filed, but nothing was done. The charges, as in past situations, eventually evaporated.(69)

In December 1992, Father Sylvestre was sent to Southdown Institute in Aurora, Ontario, for a five-day evaluation. This well-known treatment facility is designed for clergy and religious members to be treated for various afflictions. Documents from this institution show he was referred to Southdown because of allegations of sexual assault. After undergoing a battery of tests, he was released. In August 1993, Father Sylvestre, after fifty-five years as an active pastor, retired.(70)

In the same year as Sylvestre's retirement, the diocese implemented a sexual harassment policy that reaffirmed that every parish in the diocese should "be safe and healthy, poison-free places, free from sexual harassment, exploitation and abuse." The Diocese of London once again, as it had done before, vowed to deal with "any allegations of sexual harassment" promptly and "seriously discipline, to the point of termination, anyone who has contravened this policy."(71)

On July 2, 1996, Irene Duschenes and Joanne Morrison filed the first lawsuit against Father Sylvestre and the Diocese of London. The lawsuits, in the amount of $5.25 million each, claimed Sylvestre abused them while they were students at St. Ursula's School in Chatham.

Sylvestre's initial response was to emphatically declare that he had never "assaulted, abused, nor inappropriately touched" either one of these women. In October 2000, the diocese settled the lawsuit with Morrison and Deschenes for $100,000 each, but, in making this payment, it continued to deny any wrongdoing.(72)

Nine years later, after a spate of sexual abuse cases surfaced throughout North America, members of the Chatham-Kent police force descended upon the home of Sylvestre in Belle River and charged him with three counts of indecent assault, one of rape, and one of sexual intercourse with a female under fourteen years of age. In the initial stages of his interrogation by the Chatham-Kent police, Sylvestre admitted to touching the breasts of a half-dozen or more girls over the span of his pastoral career.(73)

Public opinion at the time of these early accusations was mixed. Some refused to believe that a holy man of the cloth could ever commit such heinous crimes. Others in the community believed the women filing the charges against Sylvestre were deluded, mistaken, or simply exaggerating innocent actions in order to make financial gain. Still other citizens recalled the stories they had heard from friends, neighbors, and their own children over the years. They wondered if these rumors had truly possessed some validity. In many cases, it can be reasonably assumed that many regretted their failure to listen, investigate, or question. As in all similar situations, hindsight is always twenty-twenty.

During the fall of 2005 and spring of 2006, the number of charges against the former priest continued to mount at an almost unbelievable rate. The stories that began to circulate within the community shook the average Catholic parishioner to the very bone. More and more members of the community suspected there must be a certain degree of truth to these stories. Sympathy began to shift toward the victims.

On August 3, 2006, Father Charles Sylvestre, defiantly wearing his priestly collar and looking more like a kindly grandfather than one of Canada's worst pedophiles, stood in the provincial courtroom in Chatham, Ontario, looking frail but with a hint of defiance and maybe even disdain. Lacking in any real emotion and against the hushed background of tears and a silence bespeaking years of sorrow, the disgraced pastor intoned the single word "guilty" forty-seven times.

It was one simple word repeated time after time. For some, I suppose it tended to lose its impact and power. How could this one little word ever possibly convey the depth of the pain, suffering, hurt, and guilt that these forty-seven victims harbored for so many years? How could this one word illustrate in any manner all of the heartbreak and horror that these now-older women endured when they were young, naïve, innocent, little creatures who barely resembled the women they had grown into? Nevertheless, it was at least a start. It was the first step on the long road to recovery. The healing process had finally begun.

The recognition and long road to recovery for the victims continued on August 6, 2006, when Bishop Ronald Fabbro, full of sincerity and genuine contriteness, stood in front of a packed St. Ursula's Church and spoke the words of understanding, condolence, and recognition that the forty-seven victims had longed to hear from a church official. All of it came years too late, but at least it was now being said.

Fabbro spoke of how there had been a betrayal of trust and acknowledged the sense of cynicism that existed in many of those seated in the church. He stated that they "are going to have to see the results to build that up again." He apologized for "the failure of the church to protect the victims and their families from Father Sylvestre." He offered all parishioners the reassurance that "we are now in a much better position to protect our people than we were before."(74)

Fabbro went to great pains to stress to those present that the diocese's practice of dealing with sexual abuse within the Catholic Church had radically changed since the time of Sylvestre and that no longer would a "culture of secrecy and cover-up" exist within the church. He underlined this key point by admitting publicly that Bishop John Sherlock did allow a suspected pedophile priest to continue in his role as a pastor, despite a complaint of sexual abuse in 1989.

In every parish within the Diocese of London, a written, official apology was read in which the scourge of sexual abuse would no longer be allowed to exist in any corner of the diocese. Fabbro also stated, "Once we get an accusation against a priest, we will remove him from ministry until the investigation is complete."(75)

No one could doubt the stated sincerity of Bishop Fabbro, but some victims still harbored doubts and wondered if these fine words represented a real change in church policy or if it were another example of smoke and mirrors designed to convince the skeptical. Many wondered if the church would indeed adhere to the ideal that, as Fabbro stated on that warm day in August, there was truly "no room left in the church for this kind of thinking."

Many of those assembled in churches throughout the diocese heard Fabbro's words that day and hoped for the best, but they also carefully considered the past. The fact that other Catholic bishops in other dioceses in other parts of North America and the world had stated the same old thing and then followed the same "deny, deny, deny" policy when new cases of sexual abuse surfaced lurked in the back of many a slightly cynical mind.

Fabbro made no mention of a booklet (*From Pain to Hope*) produced by the Canadian Catholic Council of Bishops in 1992 (following the Mount Cashel incidents of sexual abuses) that had been described as "a landmark study" designed to provide clear, systematic, and effective ways and means of preventing sexual abuse. It also was designed to provide specific directions for the care of victims as well as the administrative procedure to be used in cases of sexual abuse by the clergy. If the items in this document had truly been taken seriously and had been put into widespread practice in 1992, why was it necessary for Fabbro to state them in 2006 as if they were new revelations for a new direction within the Catholic Church?

Nevertheless, Bishop Fabbro had said all the right things and made an honest attempt to reach out to the victims. He vowed he had "heard the cries and pains of the victims, their anger and despair, and their demand that the church ensure that no other innocent children and young people are ever abused by a Catholic priest." Fabbro followed up on his promise to ensure that Father Sylvestre was dismissed from the priesthood by journeying to Rome and having exploratory meetings with authorities responsible for such actions in September 2006.(76)

On October 6, Father Charles Sylvestre stood before Justice Bruce Thomas in Chatham, Ontario, and heard his sentencing. He was told he must provide a DNA sample and his name would be placed in the registry of national sex offenders. He was also informed he was prohibited from owning firearms. His jail sentence, owing to his advanced years, short life expectancy, and fragile health, was set at three years in a federal penitentiary.

In sentencing Sylvestre, Justice Thomas referred to the priest's perverted cravings that were almost insatiable. He mused, "Justice is, at the best of times, an elusive commodity." He pondered aloud as to how anyone could truly attain justice in a situation such as this one.

"There is nothing I can say and nothing I can do to make matters right for you."

Sylvestre's conviction gave the aged priest a disturbing distinction. He was identified as one of the worst pedophile priests in Canadian history in a career that spanned unabated decades of abuse. The number of his known victims is close to fifty, but those who are yet to come forward or those who are too ashamed to ever do so could reach into the hundreds.

As 2006 ended, the Diocese of London began the long, painful, and costly process of dealing with the many lawsuits against them that resulted from the Sylvestre molestations over the previous forty years. In preparation for these cases, the diocese put up the traditional bishop's home in London, Ontario, for sale. When the house (the Bishop's Palace) went on sale in February 2007, the Catholic Church issued a statement through Communications Director Ron Pickersgill, indicating "proceeds from the sale of the property will be used to pay for sexual abuse claims."(77)

Subsequent news articles quoted Pickersgill contradicting himself, stating "We [Diocese of London] have been looking at the idea of selling the house for many years now." Rob Talach, a lawyer for many of the abuse victims, accused the Diocese of "being insensitive to sexual abuse victims by publicly saying the historic home is being sold to cover the expense of civil claims."(78)

In August 2008, the Diocese of London, through another spokesman, Mark Atkinson, stated that he didn't remember the Diocese of London giving the excuse of lawsuits as a reason for selling the bishop's home. Atkinson said the house was sold because it "was old and needed extensive repairs" and "the insurance companies representing the Diocese of London" would pay for "most of the lawsuits" brought against the Diocese of London by sexual abuse victims.

The blatant, contradictory statements by spokesmen for the Diocese of London served to weaken their already-tarnished public image and evoke feelings of mistrust among, not only those intimately involved, but the general public as well, who saw these statements as highly suspicious.

Further fuel was added to this fire when the mayor of Sarnia Mike Bradley, in an interview with CBC radio, stated, "Civil litigation against the church was a factor in the closing of three dozen churches within the Diocese of London, including St. Peter's in Sarnia."(79)

Diane Gauthier, one of Sylvestre's victims from Sarnia, responded to Bradley's statements, "I find it offensive that he is placing blame for the closing of churches on sexual abuse victims who have sought compensation for the injustices they suffered."

Bradley then stated, "I have the greatest of sympathy for the victims, and I was merely stating the fact that civil litigation against the church is a contributing factor in church closings."

The Diocese of London nor Mayor Mike Bradley did not state that, if Catholic Churches were being forced to close and attendance at Catholic Churches within the Diocese of London (and throughout North America) was down, it may very well have reflected the disapproval, disappointment, and possibly even disgust among Catholic parishioners with not only priests like Sylvestre, but the dismal track record of the Diocese of London and Catholic Church in general in adequately, honestly, and compassionately dealing with its many sexual abuse victims.

Before 2006 ended, the diocese, in a statement possibly designed to prove their sincerity, announced it had found copies of three witness statements dating from October 1962 that had the impact of further condemning the Diocese of London of the time. If not exactly a smoking gun, it certainly reinforced the views of those who maintained the Catholic Church, as well as the local police in Sarnia, knew of Sylvestre's pedophile behavior long before the 1990s.

The documents consisted of transcribed interviews with three girls who told police how Father Sylvestre had improperly fondled them. He had on at least one occasion exposed himself while he was a priest in Sarnia. Officials from the Diocese of London claimed they had no idea as to how or when the witness statements came into their possession. (80)

In 2006, in response to a pointed question from the media, Fabbro admitted the possibility that these documents could have been deliberately hidden. Clearly, someone in authority, whether it be church officials or police investigators, knew there was a distinct possibility that a pedophilic pastor was abusing children as early as 1962.

As a direct result of these documents being released, a total of twenty-one lawsuits on behalf of twenty-one women sexually assaulted by Father Sylvestre from the 1950s to the 1980s were brought against a number of institutions. Named in these lawsuits that allege sexual abuse by the Catholic priest when he was a pastor in Windsor, Bluewater (Sarnia), Chatham, and Pain Court, Ontario, are:

Diocese of London
Windsor-Essex Catholic School Board
St. Clair Catholic District School Board
French Catholic School Board for Southwestern Ontario
Order of Grey Nuns
Sarnia Police Department

All named for their failure to prevent the sexual abuse. The lawsuits allege the majority of defendants knew, or should have known, that Father Sylvestre was sexually abusing young girls. Allegations against the Sarnia police department include failure to pursue charges, despite being notified of specific instances of assault in 1962.(81) Directly related to the previous statement, the suit maintains that the Grey Nuns, who taught the children involved in the abuse at that time, punished the children who made the complaint instead of listening to their concerns and doing something about it.

While lawsuits, accusations, and denials ushered in the year 2007, the Diocese of London continued with its plans to prove they were sincere in their vows to overthrow shrouds of secrecy and tear down barriers involving sexual abuse. They hosted their first sexual abuse workshop at Visitation Parish in Comber, Ontario. Approximately one hundred and sixty-five people attended. Father Eugene Roy of Immaculate Conception Parish in Pain Court commented that he saw the meeting as "a real sign of support to the bishop's efforts in dealing with such a sensitive matter."(82)

Bishop Fabbro required all diocesan leaders, such as priests and deacons, to attend the Comber workshop. The day after the Comber meeting, the Diocese of London announced it would allot $44,000 to aid in the counseling of those victims of clergy sexual abuse within their parishes. On January 22, 2007, less than a week after the Comber workshop, Father Charles Sylvestre, in failing health almost since his incarceration, died of natural causes in Kingston Regional Hospital after being taken there from Millhaven Penitentiary. According to officials, he was taken from his cell at the penitentiary to the hospital, where he died alone as the cold winds of a Kingston winter blew angrily outside his window. His death brought a lonely end to a career that encompassed a half-century of unabated sexual abuse.

Sylvestre's death elicited a variety of responses from the victims. Some felt his death brought a certain amount of closure to the case; others regarded it as a sad day. Others stated they were in a state of shock, but hoped the war on sexual abuse would not die with the death of this priest abuser.

Chatham-Kent Crown Attorney Paul Bailey, relentless in his pursuit and prosecution of Sylvestre, expressed a certain degree of sorrow upon hearing of the priest's death. He stated that there is "no joy for anyone dying in prison." He stated that his passing served only to add "an added layer of tragedy" to an already tragic series of unfortunate events. (83)

Lou Ann, sitting in her home and staring silently out at the dismal January morning, broke her silence and attempted to summarize and qualify her mixed reactions:

> I feel sorry for his family, but I cannot in my heart find a great deal of compassion for him. I hoped that he would die in jail, but not this soon. I still feel that he had other questions to answer, but his death now negates any chance of him shedding light on his actions. The only solace I take in his death is that he will now have to meet his maker and face the ultimate judge. I cannot imagine a just God looking favorably upon this man's life.

Endnotes

53) Interview with Lou Ann Soontiens, April 2007.

54) Timeline: Charles Sylvestre and The Roman Catholic Diocese of London Ontario. CBC News: the fifth estate - The Good Father Timeline Feb. 28, 2007 <http://www.cbc.ca/fifth/goodfather/timeline.html>.

55) Fabian M. Saleh, Albert J. Grudzinskas, John W. Bradford, Sex Offenders: Identification, Risk Assessment, Treatment and Legal Issues (Oxford University Press, 2009) : 330-331.

56) Timeline: Charles Sylvestre and the Roman Catholic Diocese of London, Ontario. CBC News: The fifth estate - The Good Father Timeline Feb. 28th, 2007 <htttp://www.cbc.fifth/goodfather/timeline.html>.

57) Trevor Wilhelm, "To Hell And Back Sylvestre's Victims Silenced, Kept In The Dark", The Windsor Star, Nov. 2, 2006.

58) Peter Lauwers, Communications Office Diocese of London - Legal Counsel For The Diocese of London. <http://MEDIA/Sylvestre/Our Understanding of the FAxts.wpd.>

59) Trevor Wilhelm, "To Hell And Back".

60) Trevor Wilhelm, 'To Hell And Back".

61) Peter Lauwers, Communications Office Diocese Of London.

62) Peter Lauwers, Communications Office Diocese of London.

63) Timeline: Charles Sylvestre and the Roman Catholic Diocese of London Ontario. CBC News: the fifth estate.

64) Trevor Wilhelm, "Victim Ignored", Chatham Daily News, January 31, 2007.

65) Trevor Wilhelm, "To Hell and Back" .

66) Diocese of London, "What We Have Done In Our Diocese - A Chronological List", January 17th, 2007.

67) Diocese of London, "What We Have Done In Our Diocese".

68) Diocese of London, "What We Have Done".

69) Timeline: Charles Sylvestre and the Roman Catholic Diocese of London Ontario. CBC News : the fifth estate.

70) Timeline: Charles Sylvestre and the Roman Catholic Diocese of London Ontario. CBC News: the fifth estate.

71) Timeline: Charles Sylvestre and the Roman Cathlic Diocese of London Ontario. CBC News : the fifth estate.

72) Timeline: Charles Sylvestre and the Roman Catholic Diocese of London Ontario. CBC News : the fifth estate.

73) CBC News,"Diocese Apologizes For Failure To Protect Sexual Abuse Victims". Date Electronically Posted: August 3, 2006 Date Accessed: September 12th, 2006 <http:www.betnahrain.rg/bbs/index.pl/no frames/read/712>

74) Timeline: Charles Sylvestre and the Roman Catholic Diocese of London Ontario. CBC News: the fifth estate.

75) CBC News, "Diocese Apologizes For Failure To Protect Sexual Abuse Victims".

76) Trevor Wilhelm. "Sylvestre Continuously Relocated". The Windsor Star, August 22, 2008.

77) Erica Bajer, "Lawyer Says London Diocese Insensitive". Chatham Daily News, February 14, 2007.

78) Trevor Wilhelm, "Sale of Bishop's House". The Windsor Star, August 22, 2008.

79) Jack Poirier, "Mayors Comments Draw Fire", The Sarnia Observer, June 29th, 2007.

80) Trevor Wilhelm, Canadsia Bishop Works To Regain Trust After Pedophile Priest". The Windsor Star, November 2, 2009.

81) Timeline: Charles Sylvestre and the Roman Catholic Diocese of London Ontario. CBC News : the fifth estate.

82) Trevor Wilhelm, "Healing Begins - Diocese of London Holds First of Two Sex Abuse Seminars", Chatham Daily News, January 18, 2007.

83) Erica Bajer, "Charles Sylvestre's Death Stirs Emotions". The Chatham Daily News, January 24, 2007.

Chapter Seven

Victims, Villains, and Heroes

All the world's a stage and all the men and women merely players ... and one man in his time, plays many parts.
William Shakespeare, *As You Like It*

It can be hypothesized that, in the play of life, we can choose four main roles or have thrust them upon us. Of course, to paraphrase Shakespeare, we all play many parts throughout the course of our lives. It is a rare individual indeed who has not been forced or chosen through the course of a lifetime to assume the role of hero, villain, victim, or bystander. It can be argued quite successfully that representatives of all four are in the Father Sylvestre saga.

The Victims

The oldest-known victim of Father Sylvestre is now in her mid-sixties while the youngest is in her early thirties. Many of these individuals would resent or resist being labeled as "victims." Some see themselves as survivors; others still refer to themselves as thrivers who have endured the abuse. They have heroically risen above it and managed to live meaningful and fulfilled lives.

In most cases, the victims/survivors began Catholic elementary school as innocent and naïve girls who were impressionable and wanted to believe the best in people. All of them saw their parish priest as a sort of religious hero. He was someone to look up to, respect, listen to, and obey. After all, they instinctively knew he was somehow closely related to God; Father Sylvestre was someone they wanted to please.

In the early days of his career as a Catholic priest, Father Sylvestre was a rather handsome, quiet, and gentle man. Some of the victims spoke of an aura or glow about him when he was saying mass. Although much of this heavenly light could be attributed to the strategically placed stained glass windows near the altar, a bit of natural charisma seemed to surround the young priest.

On the surface, Sylvestre exhibited actions and characteristics that would make him appear to be an ideal pastor and shepherd for his young flock. He would take the young girls to the beach in the summertime, make a skating rink for them in the winter, host pizza parties, and take his young female charges for seemingly innocent rides in his car. The fact he did most of these activities almost exclusively with young females was rarely, if ever, seen initially in a negative light. After all, he was a man of God, was he not?(84)

Initial sexual contact with these young girls usually occurred on the school playground or in the rectory, where they were requested to volunteer in some mundane and routine church task. On the playground, he would come up behind his young female victims, casually place his hands over and down their shoulders, and fondle their small breasts. On other occasions, he would walk with them across the crowded playground with his hands improperly placed on their breasts. For more than half of the victims, this type of molestation began when the girls were only nine or ten years old.

Father Sylvestre would not hesitate to conduct his abuse in front of other girls as they were gathered around him on the playground or working on small projects for him in the rectory. His abuse was conducted in such an offhanded, casual manner that very few of his inexperienced victims ever suspected that what he was doing was wrong. After all, he was a man of God, was he not? So subtle and natural was his approach to these incidents of abuse that many of his victims would later ponder upon the distinct possibility that the actual abuse they endured was much more than they could remember with many incidents being forgotten.

According to sexual abuse researcher Michael J. Bland, Sylvestre's approach in molesting his victims was almost textbook in nature. He followed, almost perfectly, the four steps that Bland (85) says most child sexual abusers follow :

Gain the victim's trust.

Lure the victim into seemingly innocent physical contact with the molester.

Make the victim feel indebted to the molester through gifts and/or special favors, making it emotionally difficult for the victim to resist.

Confuse the victim about whether or not the sexual contact is acceptable.

In many cases, these steps would make the child appear to be compliant and cooperative. This would allow molesters like Father Sylvestre to conjure up in their twisted minds the needed illusion that the child had given his or her consent. In turn, the adult abuser sees this as providing justification for his actions. As with Lou Ann, the molester was grooming his victim in a systematic seduction that was aimed at winning the trust and confidence of a vulnerable and needy child. In many cases, when the young victims reported the abuse by Sylvestre to an adult figure, they were, like Lou Ann and many others, disbelieved. Most parents minimized or discounted their concerns, and these reactions led most of the young girls to experience a great deal of confusion and a certain amount of guilt.

Many may have felt vaguely uncomfortable with Father Sylvestre, but their trusting parents often reassured them that the good priest would never do anything wrong. After all, he was a man of God, was he not?

Many victims in the Sylvestre situation, as well as in most other recorded clergy abuse situations, would often have feelings of self-accusation. Many felt they had to bear some of the blame for this abuse. Some felt there must have been something wrong with them for not wanting to be with this popular priest who elicited such respect, admiration, and trust from their friends, teachers, and parents. Another typical victim response was a feeling of guilt over not doing enough to protect those younger than themselves from the advances of Father Sylvestre.

Victims of Father Sylvestre, like other young victims of abuse in other cases, experienced a number of psychological problems later in life, including low self-esteem, dysfunctional behavior, anxiety, depression, anger and irritability, disassociation, inability to trust others, and problems with intimacy.

In the case involving Father Porter in Massachusetts, which happened at approximately the same time as the sexual abuse by Father Sylvestre was occurring, therapists interviewing the victims reported that "people often suffer intensified psychological difficulties later in life whose origins seem to be found in sexual approaches made to them during childhood by a priest."(86)

In recounting her own problems with adult life, Lou Ann expressed fears and concerns that were typical of clergy abuse victims. In an interview with the author, Lou Ann made it very clear that, for a good portion of her life, she never felt that good things should happen to her. She often had feelings of diminished value and self-worth. For most of her life, she felt very uncomfortable with her body. She still dislikes anyone touching her.(87)

Other victims of abuse by Father Sylvestre and other clergy throughout North America reported having an inherent disrespect for any type of authority figure. This, in turn, has made it difficult for many of these victims to hold down careers or advance in their chosen professions. In the case of Lou Ann, she went from job to job throughout her life and only found a comfortable employment niche when she started her own business.

Other victims of clergy abuse developed a general distrust of the entire educational system. They not only perceived the abusive priest as part of the educational system, but also the teachers (often nuns) who did not rescue them from the clutches of the evil priest as part and parcel of the abuse.(88)

It is not possible to draw an accurate picture of a clergy abuse victim and state categorically that all abuse victims exhibit these specific characteristics. Victims in every situation, including those abused by Father Sylvestre, vary widely in their personal response to the abuse. They all developed their own personal coping strategies.

Some victims, like Lou Ann, left home early, dropped out of school, and got involved in brief, turbulent, and unhappy marriages. Others simply left the community and never returned. In their own ways, all were attempting to run away from the abuse that could never really be eluded for long. All were living with their pasts. Most expected to die with their horrible secret remaining hidden. Few expected that the man responsible would be brought to trial and exposed. He had been unaccountable for his actions throughout most of his life, so why should that fact ever change?

All victims do share at least one common trait. They wonder how their lives with regard especially to relationships, personal adjustments, and careers would have been different if Father Sylvestre had never inflicted such pain upon them. They also seek some type of closure related to their abuse that would allow the healing process to begin in a meaningful fashion. They want recognition by the community and society in general that a great wrong was done to them and the accountability available to them through the judicial system be enacted.

While a few people in the community have made some disparaging remarks about the amount of money victims are seeking through the court system, those people are missing a key point. The victims know that any amount of monetary payment will never truly repay them for their suffering, but they want society as a whole to recognize they did suffer. Large payments by the Catholic Church serve as recognition to the victims and society as a whole that the church was wrong and must now pay for their crimes and failures. The payment of the money is simply a symbolic act that allows victims to be recognized as such victims within the society that they had to live for so long in silence, sadness, and solitude.(89) When one looks at the damage done to these women, the years of suffering they had to endure in solitude, and the disruption to their entire lives, can any amount of money truly be considered just compensation?

Viewed in this light, the victims/survivors of Father Sylvestre's abuse must also be considered as heroes. They endured more than any human should have to endure for a good portion of their lives. Although many did have problems in life, jobs, and relationships and within their own psyches, the vast majority of them are, as they state in their own words, "thrivers."

Priests as Victims

It can also be argued that the majority of Catholic priests are also victims, in not only the case of Father Sylvestre, but all the other molestation cases that have occurred in North America since the 1980s. In any analysis, it cannot be stressed often enough that the vast majority of Catholic priests in North America and throughout the world are honest, hardworking, religious, principled, and good men who have unfortunately been painted with the same brush that colors the many crimes of people like Father Porter, Father Gauthe, Father Geoghan, and Father Sylvestre.

This is a very unfortunate situation. Imagine if you were the current priest at St. Ursula's Church in Chatham or any Catholic Church in North America tarnished by the deeds of a priest such as Sylvestre. How would you interact with the children at the school next door? Would you walk the playground and talk with the children? Would you pat them on the head as a gesture of acknowledgement? Would you put your arm around a student if he or she needed consoling? Would you allow yourself to be alone with a young female student?

The answers to these questions are obvious, but absolutely unfortunate. A priest should be able to do all these things and not be subject to suspicion. But I am afraid that the legacy of Sylvestre and these other pedophile priests will rein in the role of priests and move them one step further away from the youth in parishes throughout North America at a time when the world, in general, is in turmoil and priestly guidance is much needed by many of today's young.

It is even more unfortunate that these scandals occur at a time in history when there have been fewer and fewer young Catholic men entering the priesthood. The decline began in the 1960s. Forces inside as well as outside the church have conspired to deplete the numbers of priests to a dangerous low. If you add the taint of sexual deviancy to a profession that has already lost pastors due to rigid stands by the Vatican against birth control, abortion, and the ordination of women, the result is devastating.(90)

Because of these sexual crimes, the average priest in North America will suffer the slings and arrows of suspicious parents, teachers, and parishioners for a long time to come. This fact makes them very much the innocent victims of priests like Father Sylvestre as well.

They certainly did not, nor do they, suffer in the same fashion or to the same degree as the female victims of these priests, but they have and will suffer in ways that will haunt them for many years to come. We will all be the poorer for that.

Parishioners as Victims

Faithful Catholic parishioners are also victims in subtle and not-so subtle ways. Many have spent all of their lives faithfully supporting the Catholic Church from moral, spiritual, and financial points of view. Many have spent a good portion of their existence defending the church against the barbs of outsiders who were critics of the Catholic Church.

Many of these parishioners must now endure the hurtful comments initiated by the actions of priests like Father Sylvestre. Few things can be said in the face of these sexual transgressions by a man of God. Many times, a man they trusted without reservation committed these horrible, unspeakable crimes. Many parishioners must feel not only hurt, but a very real sense of absolute betrayal.

Not only must these God-fearing, loyal Catholics silently endure the embarrassment of these acts committed by their pastors, they also much watch as millions of dollars that they worked diligently to raise pay for the sins of a few. Some estimate that the Roman Catholic Church and its various insurance brokers have already paid out well over a billion dollars to victims, and the figure is climbing virtually every day.(91)

It is an unnecessary and terrible burden for the average Catholic parishioner to bear. Many have simply had enough and are leaving the church in disgust and embarrassment. Many can no longer support an institution that has so mishandled such a serious situation so many times and in so many obvious ways. They are fed up and showing their disapproval by nonattendance or joining another religion.(92)

Whatever the situation, it is obvious that disgruntled Catholic parishioners see themselves as victims of the hierarchy of the Catholic Church and are rising up in anger. No longer will they blindly accept church decisions, excuses, or directives. They are demanding accountability and responsibility from everyone from their pope to their parish priest. Obviously, the Catholic Church will never be the same. Many might argue that it is an extremely positive, if somewhat painful, outcome.

The Villains

It is difficult to label any individual involved in the Father Sylvestre abuse case as villains. It would, of course, be very easy and almost a forgone conclusion to place Father Sylvestre in the role of absolute villain, but that label is too simplistic and fails to look at the complete picture.

Unquestionably, this priest misused and abused his position in the most heinous ways possible, and he continued in his abuse for over four decades. The abuse inflicted upon these young girls who trusted him completely and saw him as God's representative can never be forgiven nor forgotten, but one could argue that he was, to a degree, a victim as well.

Charles Sylvestre was a sick man in every sense of that word. His blatant public displays of abuse could be seen as a subconscious cry for help for someone, in this case, the hierarchy of the Catholic Church, to stop him and rescue him from his own terrible illness

The term *pedophile* applies to those sexual abusers with a primary interest in children. In medical terms, pedophilia is considered to be a psychiatric disorder marked by an adult's persistent attraction to children who have not reached adolescence. Those children are usually under the age of thirteen. Most experts consider it manageable, but essentially incurable. A pedophile can learn not to act on his desires, but he cannot exorcise what basically amounts to a sexual orientation. (93)

Those abusers who experience an attraction to adolescents (ages thirteen to fifteen) are labeled as *ephebophilia*, an immature and inappropriate partner choice. It too is considered to be an aberrant sexual orientation, one that is not easily treated nor altered.

Looking at the victims of Father Sylvestre, one might speculate that he was basically a pedophile with aspects of ephebophilia. This, of course, is not a medical determination in any way, but it is simply a layperson's speculation based on the abuse inflicted upon the victims that we now know about. No matter how an experienced team of psychiatrists may, in retrospect, officially label Sylvestre's condition, I think it is fair to state that he was in need of extensive help. Many might argue that this help should have come from the Catholic Church in a decisive, immediate, and effective manner.

The fact that the Catholic Church failed to help Sylvestre and hundreds of other priests suffering from the same disease or psychological impairment throughout North America for decades leads one to speculate that the priest, who was psychologically incapable of helping himself, was not the real villain. In reality, it could be argued that it was the religious organization that ordained him as a priest and refused to rescind that decree or offer help that was the real victim.

This view is not meant to exonerate, excuse, or minimize the role Father Sylvestre played in his own demise, but it is meant to offer the possibility that what he did over four decades need not have happened to the degree to which it did. If Father Sylvestre is to be painted as a villain, it must be recognized that, at the very least, he should not be the only one in the picture.

Bystanders

Dr. William S. Cottringer wrote on the different roles people play in life. He stated, "Perhaps the weakest role a person can choose to play in life is that of a bystander."(94)

In North America, lawsuits currently cite various Catholic boards of education as being partially responsible for the sexual crimes of priests. In essence, they are accused of being bystanders who chose not to take action. Some victims argue these boards of education should have been aware of these molestations and history of these priest predators and taken appropriate action to remove the child from the grasp of these offenders and place them in a safe educational environment.

Following this point of view, one could also argue that there are some childcare workers, teachers, elected officials, and police officers who could be deemed to play, to a greater or lesser extent, the role of bystander. All kinds of people who hold public trust, from childcare workers to elected officials, seem to cower when dealing with child sexual abuse by a priest. Teachers in Catholic schools (nuns or laypeople) often fail to notice that the kindly priest is always pulling Johnny or Mary out of class or children seem to vanish when he (the priest) approaches.

In the case of Father Sylvestre, the same pattern seemed to hold true. Lou Ann (as well as other Sylvestre victims) often wondered why her teachers did not come to her aid and intercede on her behalf although she was sure that many must have had their suspicions.

There does not seem to be any record currently available that would indicate that any social worker or childcare worker ever officially suspected or reported any type of sexual abuse by Father Sylvestre. There seems to be three recorded instances where sexual molestation of a minor was reported to police in the communities where Father Sylvestre was a pastor prior to 2003, but nothing was done, as the investigating officers decided that the victim lacked credibility.(95)

In all of these examples involving Father Sylvestre and his victims, there is nothing unique nor sinister in their nature. These same reactions have occurred in almost every community throughout North America where a pedophile priest has operated. It does not mean that these officials are irresponsible or not doing their jobs. It has more to do with the respect and trust that we have as a society toward Catholic priests and the respect that society as a whole has had for the Catholic Church.

In hindsight, many might take to task childcare workers, teachers, fellow priests, and the police for not having taken action sooner and in a more proactive fashion. If they made mistakes, they were ones of omission rather than of commission. Hopefully, these individuals would act much differently in the future when faced with similar situations. Oftentimes, a bystander is simply someone who needs to be prodded into action.

The teachers at the schools where Father Sylvestre was a pastor and had contact with many children may bear the most responsibility. However, as has been discussed before, the courage to actually accuse a priest of such crimes may have been simply beyond the capabilities of even the most worldly-wise teaching sister. They may have naïvely believed that no man of God would ever harm an innocent child. If they truly believed this, as it would seem most likely that they did, they were certainly not alone.

Most of the parents, parishioners, and average person in the community who encountered the genial, soft-spoken priest never suspected Father Sylvestre either. As in many other situations throughout North America where a priest was involved in pedophile activities, it is only in retrospect that the many people who had contact with the offending pastors look back on words, actions, and events and only now see something sinister in that which once seemed so innocent.

We all live with the demons of what we could have done, should have done, and might have done, but these actions do not automatically classify us as villains or even irresponsible bystanders. Rather, they simply show us to be human beings who rarely live lives free of mistakes or errors in judgment.

Once again, there seems to be only one clear-cut villain or, if we wish to be a bit kinder, bystander in this sordid matter. Incident after incident dealing with sexual predator priests seem to strongly point toward the Catholic Church. In the final analysis, the hierarchy of the Catholic Church must wear this mantle of shame in not only the local situation involving Father Sylvestre, but in the hundreds of other modern sexual abuse cases throughout North America as well as throughout history.

The Heroes

As in many of the other clergy abuse cases that transpired throughout North America since the 1980s, there are some marked similarities when one looks at the various characters, organizations, and institutions involved.

The police in most of the clergy sexual abuse cases throughout North America since the 1980s have displayed remarkable similarities. They have almost, without fail, been initially timid, reluctant, and hesitant to investigate the Catholic Church when cases of sexual abuse have been first brought to their attention. In Sarnia (1962) and Chatham (1989), the police did not pursue Father Sylvestre as they felt the complainant was not credible. In the latter case, the detective assigned to investigate the case was also a parishioner at St. Ursula's Church in Chatham and knew Father Sylvestre.

According to Bruni and Burkett, they explain the hesitancy of civil authorities to act in these cases is not a conspiracy, but simply a "subtle collusion borne of respect bordering on awe for an institution whose power seemed to transcend the temporal. It was willful but rarely conscious."(96)

Out of respect for the clergy and Catholic Church, police as well as other officials were often reluctant to drag a priest into court. They would rather have left him to the discipline of the church. Like most of us, they wanted to believe the Catholic Church had an effective and efficient way of dealing with the offenders as well as the victims. We all had a lot to learn.

The Catholic Church exudes an aura of power. Although this power in modern times is more myth than reality, it nevertheless has a carryover impact. Oftentimes, when the police did pursue an abusive clergy member, other law enforcement agencies, prosecutors, or judges stonewalled them.

Locally, the Chatham-Kent Police Department began to take things seriously in 2003. Once they began, things moved efficiently and effectively. Inspector George Flickwert and Detective Constable Kate McCarthur performed admirably in not only pressing charges against Sylvestre, but in dealing with the victims as well.

Although the local police in Chatham may have been a bit reluctant to initially get involved in 1989, the Chatham Kent Police force, led by Flikweert and McCarthur, pursued the eighty-four-year-old Sylvestre with a great deal of vim and vigor. The various victims (now conservatively estimated to number in excess of eighty) are quite unanimous in their admiration for Kate McCarthur, who obviously used a great deal of sensitivity, innate intelligence, and sincere compassion when dealing with the victims.

Although many victims might justifiably protest that the police reaction was much too little and much too late to stop Sylvestre when he was actually abusing, the actions taken by the 2003 Chatham Kent Police Services was thorough, efficient, and effective. Many of the victims cited McCarthur as being particularly understanding, caring, and considerate. Her hard work and dedication in this case earned her the Excellence in Performance Award from the Ontario Women in Law Enforcement in May 2007. Placing Flikweert and especially McCarthur in the heroes category of this case seems to be very appropriate.(97)

When Father Dino Cinel of New Orleans was accused of running a kiddy-porn cottage industry out of the basement of his Catholic Church in 1988, there was a great deal of hesitancy in bringing charges against him. This reluctance was directly attributed to Harry Connick Sr. (father of the famous singer) who was not only the district attorney of New Orleans, but a devout Catholic and member of Cinel's parish. Although deemed to be an excellent DA and a crusader against pornography, Connick stonewalled efforts to prosecute Father Cinel at every stage due largely to an intense desire to protect the church.(98)

Connick's slow and obstinate behavior in order to protect the reputation of the Catholic Church was not a singular incident. Examples of prosecutors who took similar actions in situations where Catholic priests were suspected of sexual abuse are numerous in North America.(99)

While this reluctance to prosecute may have been the case in other places in North America, it definitely was not the case with Father Sylvestre in Chatham-Kent. It was not the case here, due chiefly to the efforts of one man who, in almost everyone's estimation, must be considered to be a hero.

Chatham-Kent Crown Attorney Paul Bailey felt an immediate and real empathy for the victims of Father Sylvestre and expressed in thought, deed, action, and speech all of the outrage, anger, disillusionment, and betrayal felt by the victims as well as the entire community. He saw the evil in not only this priest, but also the careless disregard for the institution that allowed him to freely victimize young, innocent girls for decades.

Bailey was like a pit bull let loose. Old arguments, empty promises, or lame excuses were not going to cower him. He saw through the sham of the Catholic Church's method of dealing with its sexually abusing priests. He was adamant that these sins be made public so the courts as well as the general public could censure the church hierarchy and demand change.

In essence, Paul Bailey became the loud voice of the many quiet victims who were forced to remain silent for so many long and torturous years. He became their strong, vibrant champion who put the unspeakable crimes committed against them into powerful words and images. Someone was now actually speaking for them.

He was pulling back the dark curtain that had shrouded their lives for so many years, and he was casting light upon these crimes. It was the light of truth and compassion. He was their knight; he was bearing their standard. He was standing up and stating in a clear voice that bespoke outrage, betrayal, and incredulity. His voice spoke for them and us. They were no longer complainants who lacked credibility. He made them feel that their stories would finally not only be heard, but, more importantly, believed.

The average citizen, regardless of religious affiliation, liked it when he allowed his emotions to show. They liked it when anger colored his statements. They cheered him on when he questioned those who should have listened, responded, and cared. He refused to mouth the media-appropriate phrases and words of concern, care, and compassion. His feelings were genuine, real, raw, and absolutely compelling. He demanded justice for these victims. He imbued a sometimes rather stodgy, robotlike job with life, dignity, and zeal of an avenging angel.

When he issued statements bluntly telling the Catholic Church that it must change and he chastised the police for not listening and investigating years before, we were beside him, cheering him on and wanting to know the answers.

He was passionate and outraged. He took the robbing of the innocence of these forty-seven young girls as personal. His passion came from deep within because it was real and natural. He reassured the victims that they were worthy, worthwhile human beings who had been used and abused and were now seeking justice. He told the world that it was a justice that they richly deserved and one that had long been denied.

Bailey's greatest gift to these victims was that he represented society, the society that had so long ignored them and society that forced them to remain quiet about their pasts. The victims saw him as that parent, teacher, and adult who had never stood up on their behalf. He finally confronted Father Sylvestre and the Catholic Church and demanded that their pain and suffering be recognized.

The lawyers for Ledroit Beckett Litigation Lawyers might be placed in the hero category. Some would argue that their interest in these sexual abuse cases should be classified as purely monetary and financially motivated. As a result, it would not fit into any of these arbitrary categories. But it can also be argued that, although there certainly was the monetary motivation incentive at work, they also seemed to take the plight of the women they represented in these sexual abuse situations to heart. It became much more than mere financial gain. They saw the wrongs done by Father Sylvestre, Diocese of London, and Catholic Church in general. They wanted to intercede for these women. They wanted to help empower these women and give them dignity, respect, and a new start in lives that had been badly shattered as innocent children.

One lawyer for Ledroit Beckett seemed to take the civil suits against Father Sylvestre even more personally than some of the others did. In discussing the case with the author, Rob Talach recounted in shades of disbelief, sometimes bordering upon anger, that he was a teenager living in Pain Court, a short distance from Immaculate Conception Church, when Father Sylvestre was accused of molesting at least three young girls.

Although it would have been impossible for him to know about the situation at that time or for him as a teenager to do anything meaningful about it, he seemed determined to go back in time and rectify a wrong that he could not have corrected at the time. It obviously made an impact upon him and inspired him with zeal and a passion to bring to light, among other things, the pattern of shuffling by the diocese, where Sylvestre was moved from parish to parish as complaints arose.

"There's a horrific track record here," Tallach said, "and it would be nice to bring it out in court."

The law firm of Ledroit Beckett made money on these sexual abuse cases, but, in my mind, they earned every cent and worked diligently and well above the call of duty to bring some dignity, closure, and justice into the lives of those women abused by Sylvestre who were not able to achieve these things on their own. I know Lou Ann and many of the other abused women consider these lawyers to be heroes. In the final analysis, that is reason enough to consider them as such.

The victims of Father Sylvestre's sexual abuse are not only victims, but survivors and, last but not least, heroes. They were the ones who would not allow Father Sylvestre's sins to go unpunished, even though they knew their pursuit would cost them dearly. They pursued him with a zeal that must have appeared to be ill-advised and hopeless. They would not give in and give up. They told their stories repeatedly to anyone they thought might listen and advance their cause.

They relived the pain, humiliation, and suffering so we would know and they might finally be purged of that which had plagued them in solitude for so many hurtful years. They did not rest until society clearly recognized and acknowledged they had been done wrong by not only a man and a priest, but by the Catholic Church and, to a certain extent, society as a whole.

One definition of heroes describes them as people who "dream big, translate their dreams into concrete goals, work hard to leave their legacy, remain flexible, and never quit." This seems to be a very accurate description of Lou Ann and all the other women molested by Father Sylvestre for so many years and in so many places.(100)

Few of us would possess the same sort of inner strength and fortitude to do what they did and do what they continue to do. Those people looking for female heroes in today's world need to look no further than these brave women.

A Morality Play Too Often Performed

Incidents of sexual abuse by clerics throughout North America seem to follow almost scripted scenes. More often than not, these involve the same characters in the same roles. In many ways, one might characterize these oft-repeated scenarios as a form of the traditional morality play.

The traditional morality play was a type of traditional allegory in which the protagonist is met by the personification of various moral attributes who try to persuade the audience into choosing the godly, moral life over one of evil and immorality. In these plays, there were the protagonists, antagonists, and usual supporting cast of characters. The type of morality play that transpired around the sexual abuse scandals within the Catholic Church was performed in many North American venues and usually involved the same cast of characters. We had the sexually abused victims, the villains in the form of the sexually abusive priests and the Catholic Church, and the heroes who somehow brought these crimes to light, put a halt to them, and rescued the victims from further abuse.

Unfortunately, the audience (Catholic parishioners, society, and so forth) never got the play's message. The audience, like the Catholic Church officials, missed the moral lesson about learning to think, act, and operate in a moral, principled fashion and pressing for moral change and action.

They were not able, or possibly were never allowed, to clearly understand the lesson and apply it to the next set of plays that were, unfortunately, being acted out with seemingly increasing regularity.

They did not see the whole picture. Subsequently, they did not attempt to stop the victims from acting again. They were bystanders lacking the will, power, and understanding to change things.

One wonders how many more of these morality plays must be tragically acted out before the audience truly, completely, and absolutely gets the point and the moral message. The audience must rise up, take control, and force changes in a centuries-old institution that has seemingly lost touch with what is right and what is wrong. If they choose once again to ignore the lesson, choose to trust in church leaders and their outmoded policies, and choose to trust the male leaders who are woefully out of touch with life, then there will be many more victims like Lou Ann. Future scandals will continue to rock the Catholic Church and ultimately cause it to self-destruct.

Endnotes

84) Jane Sims, "Betrayal of Trust", London Free Press, January 17, 2007.

85) Marie Fortune and Merle E. Longwood eds.., Sexual Abuse In The Catholic Church (The Haworth Pastoral Press, 2003) : 27.

86) Frank Bruni and Elinor Burkett, A Gospel of Shame (New York: Harper Collins Publishers Inc., 2002) : 21.

87) Author's Interview With Lou Ann Soontiens, May 2008.

88) Jane Sims, Betrayal of Trust".

89) Frank Bruni and Elinor Burkett, A Gospel of Shame : 33.

90) Marie Fortune and Merle E. Longwoods eds., Sexual Abuse In The Catholic Church.

91) Frank Bruni and Elinor Burkett, A Gospel of Shame.

92) John Garvey, "Why People Leave The Church". Commonweal - A Revue of Religion, Politics and Culture. Date of Electronic Publication: April 6, 2007 Date Accessed: May 25, 2006. <http://www.commonwealmagazine.org/article.php3?id_article>.

93) Frank Bruni and Elinor Burkett, A Gospel of Shame : 46.

94) William S. Cottinger, Heroes, Villains, Victims and Bystanders. Date of Publication: February 12, 2007 Date Accessed: April 15, 2009. <http://www.selfgrowth.com/article/heroes_villains_victims_bystandershtml>.

95) Timeline: Charles Sylvestre and the Roman Catholic Diocese of London, Ontario. CBC News: the fifth estate - The Good Father - Timeline Feb. 28, 2007 <http:www.cbc.ca/fifth/godfather/timeline.html.

96) Frank Bruni and Elinor Burkett, A Gospel of Shame :53

97) Erica Bajer, "Detectives Honoured For Work On Sylvestre Case", Chatham Daily News, February 14, 2007.

98) Jeffrey Murrell, "The Monster and the Boys", in Elysian Fiels Lost, Chapter 6 Part II. Date of Electronic Publication: March 3, 1990 Date Accessed: April 4, 2007
<http://www.seabrite.com/author/murrell/elysian/htm.>

99) Jeffrey Murrell, "The Monster and the Boys".

100) Jeffrey Murrell, "The Monster and the Boys".

Chapter Eight

Restoring the Faith in the Catholic Church

We had the experience, but missed the meaning.
The Four Quartets, T.S. Eliot

A key tenet in this look at the Catholic Church and the issue of sexual abuse within its ranks is the undeniable fact that the Catholic Church's credibility has been severely damaged and greatly diminished. On more than one occasion, it has been pointed out that the Catholic Church is generally not terribly supportive of victims. In many cases, it would appear that church officials would rather take the side of the villains (offending Catholic priests) at the expense of the young victims of sexual abuse.

Long-standing and faithful parishioners have suffered a great deal and feel they have been betrayed by a church they love and have spent their entire lives defending and supporting from a moral and financial point of view.

Some people, within and outside the Catholic Church, feel the church's handling of the sexual abuse victims across North America demonstrates very clearly the Machiavellian adage that "power corrupts and absolute power corrupts absolutely." The disregard by the Catholic Church of proper legal procedure in these criminal cases leaves many people with a terrible taste in their mouths.

In many of these sexual abuse scandals, the Catholic Church gave the appearance of being too concerned with the business of being an institution rather than their stated mission of being an entity dedicated to loving, caring, and human spirituality.

The Catholic Church must come to terms with these issues. If it wishes to survive as a meaningful and important spiritual guide, it must make some radical systematic changes that may be anathema to the very nature of this ancient institution, but are absolutely necessary for survival in the twenty-first century. The Catholic Church often argues:

- The sexual abuse problem within the church has been blown out of proportion. They counter criticisms with the view that the number of sexual abusers within their clerical numbers is very small and account for less than 4 percent of all priests.
- The percentage of their priests who are sexual abusers is about the same as that percentage in the community as a whole. Although more research needs to be done to prove or disprove this view, the actual numbers and ratio is really not that important. The real issue is how the officials and hierarchy of Catholic Church dealt with the victims of these sexual abuses in almost every situation.

While it may very well be true that it is only a few rotten apples in the harvest that spoil the entire barrel, they once again miss the point or are deliberately deflecting the real reason for the problem. It may not be the fruit within the container that is the essential problem. Rather, it may be the container that holds the fruit and those who choose that fruit and pack it into such containers that is the real source of concern.

The real damage that has been done to the Catholic Church rests not so much with the priests themselves. Rather, it is with the inhumane, insensitive, heartless fashion in which the victims were often treated. Church officials typically discounted and dismissed their claims, feelings, and situations in an imperious, impersonal fashion that clearly sent the message to society as well as the victims and their families that the reputation of the Catholic Church and its priests were the important aspects in the whole scheme of things. Victims were usually not much more than annoying inconveniences that should simply suck it up, shut up, and go away.

Statements by Pope Paul II as late as 1993 blamed the sensation-hungry North American media for exaggerating the problem by reporting on the large number of sexual abuse cases in North America. Describing it as a media witch hunt, he dismissed the stories and scolded the media as a whole for pursuing stories that were "opposed to the pursuit of the moral good."

Statements like the preceding by the supreme leader of the worldwide Catholic Church does not help to ease or solve the sexual abuse problem in any fashion. Nor does the usual official statement by church officials that offending priests must use prayer rather than treatment as the most important path to reconciliation help restore faith in the Roman Catholic Church.

Victims, as well as many people in North American society, want public confessions, public apologies, jail time, and meaningful lump sum payments to victims like Lou Ann and the thousands of other victims who have suffered so much in such deafening silence for so long.

The large scandal and negative publicity created by the issue of sexual abuse by pedophilia and ephebophilia priests within the Catholic Church, especially in North America, cannot and must not be summarily dismissed by church officials. The issue will not go away. It is ridiculously dangerous to believe that all offending priests within the Catholic Church have been rooted out and no new ones will be ordained, especially if the exact same conditions exist within the structure of the church.

The reported incidents of sexual abuse among priests within the Catholic Church may very well turn out to be the most devastating and extensive issue the church has ever faced. If it does not respond in a manner that acknowledges the seriousness of the situation, it may very well lose its position, power, and spiritual influence. This is not a desirable situation for anyone. As this book has stressed throughout, the Catholic Church has much to offer if it can change with the times and become a more relevant moral force in society.

It will be a massive, frightening, and gut-wrenching task for this venerable, old institution to change many of its centuries-old approaches, but I firmly believe it has the capability to do so. This would greatly enhance its image, influence, and positive impact throughout the world.

The Catholic Church is at that crisis point in its existence. It is just as important for parishes that have never been touched by such scandals to get together and determine possible strategies to implement in the event of even the slightest hint of this type of abuse occurring within their church.

These individual church committees could also serve as a valuable resource for the entire Catholic Church as it attempts to address the problem from a universal perspective, as they hopefully critically review the entire structure of the Catholic Church. The more individuals involved in the review and revision of the church, the better the ultimate result will be.

The following points, presented in no particular order, are humbly and very respectfully presented here as suggestions. I do not presume to have all the answers, nor do I want to minimize the enormous task it represents in changing aspects of the Catholic Church that have been so ingrained for such a long time.

The suggestions represent not only my personal observations, but a good cross section of what many observers (for example, Church reformers, Catholic priests, victims, law enforcement agencies, parishioners, and the average person) have expressed at various times in response to this tragic situation within the Catholic Church.

The reality of the situation is that, unless issues like these presented in the list as well as many others, are seriously addressed by concerned Catholics, the important, vital, and powerful force for good that is inherent within the Catholic Church may cease to exist.

Many readers will certainly agree with the need for a serious self-examination by church officials. This time though, it must be sincere, all-encompassing and it must seek meaningful input from its longtime loyal parishioners who, like many of the victims of sexual abuse, have been ignored and marginalized for much too long.

A Starting Point: Suggested Changes

- In cases of sexual abuse among its clergy, the Catholic Church must stop allowing church lawyers to set the tone and mold the response. It must organize the strategies with regard to abused victims. Parish priests must be allowed and encouraged to talk with and administer to victims of sexual abuse. The concept that, each time a parish priest talks to a victim, it costs the Catholic Church big bucks must be forsaken as a heartless and barbaric practice.

- The reputation of the Catholic Church and its priests must never be allowed to supersede the needs of the victims in sexual abuse situations.
- Bishops must stop acting as business managers or CEOs intent on secrecy, church image, and maintenance of financial resources within the Catholic Church. The victims and their needs must take precedent over all else.
- Standardized policies and set procedures need to be established for all Catholic Churches that address the needs of the victims. These procedures should include, among others, counseling and legal advice. Problems arise when different diocese have different approaches to dealing with victims. This hodgepodge approach creates a climate where a fair, well-thought-out response is sometimes obscured or tainted in the eyes of the public, despite the best of intentions by individual parishes or dioceses.
- At the first suggestion of sexual impropriety among members of church clerics, the Catholic Church must swing into action and come to the aid and defense of the victims. The skeptical, challenging stance that has often dominated responses with regard to accusations made by children against priests must be stopped. The church must react as if accusations have some merit and respond accordingly until the opposite is proven.
- A full financial picture that is all-inclusive and complete must be presented to parishioners. This financial statement must accurately address the actual monies that have been spent in the defense of offending priests, as well as court costs, public relations expenses, assessment and treatment costs, counseling for victims, court-ordered settlements, and private deals cut with victims and their families.
- Parishioners at all Catholic Churches must be allowed to have a definite and meaningful way of contributing to the actions taken by Catholic leaders when dealing with issues of sexual abuse. The average layperson within the Catholic Church has a great deal to offer in the form of advice and keeping the church officials on the correct moral path. Catholic leaders must no longer regard the average parishioner as a mindless child who has nothing to offer. In today's world, many parishioners are well-educated, experienced,

resourceful, and insightful. They want to be involved. The days of the passive parishioner listening without questioning and blindly obeying the parish priest, bishop, or even the pope are over.

- The parishioners must have much more say in the choosing of their parish priest. There must be some assurances that the candidates presented for their decision have undergone some sort of psychological testing to ensure there are no obvious signs nor suspected history of pedophilia or ephebophilia.
- The Catholic Church must develop and implement a policy designed to, when necessary, defrock priests. This process should be transparent, expedient, and standardized. If a court of law convicts a priest of sexual abuse, he should be summarily defrocked. This occurs in the teaching profession, legal profession, and other professional bodies. Should this same process not be followed within the Catholic Church? Ordination should not trump the correct, proper, moral, and logical thing to do.
- Diocese councils that include laity among its members might consider making a symbolic statement by quickly implementing a sexual abuse prevention program (for example, good-touch/bad touch, the two-deep rule, and so forth) in all Catholic schools, religious education programs, church youth groups, training of altar servers, and any other program in which church personnel have regular contact with minors.
- The Catholic Church must come to terms with the fact that its greatest weakness may be its rigid hierarchical system that has created a definite class system within its very structure. The pope is above the bishop, who is above the priest, who is above the common man, who is above the common woman, who is above the child. This type of system bestows privilege, power, respect, and dominance in a descending order. Based entirely on position and the role they have been assigned to play within the structure of the institution, actual deeds, merits, actions, and personality are forced to play a very secondary role. Priests who sexually molest see children, who are on the lowest rung in this power ladder, as the weakest and most vulnerable within the system, so they are likely victims. In addition, the hierarchical system of the church protects those who should be punished. In this rigid power system,

it is difficult to accuse those who are above you and maintain your position.
- A painful but much-needed examination needs to be undertaken to examine, question, debate, and defend issues within the Catholic Church that have never been examined in a realistic and progressive, open-minded fashion. Unbiased, critical, and all-encompassing examinations must take place concerning such traditional hot-button issues like mandatory celibacy, women in the priesthood, and the issues addressed or not addressed during training at Catholic seminaries.
- At its highest levels, the Catholic Church must examine the possibility of allowing women to embrace the mantle of priesthood. Celibacy and a woman's role in the church are sticking points in the minds of many Catholics and non-Catholics alike. Once again, a reasonable, objective, and open-minded examination would go a long way to enhance the image of the Catholic Church as being a progressive, enlightened institution capable of making changes when necessary.
- Although there is much debate about the relationship between mandatory celibacy and the incident of sexual abuse, there needs to be an honest, transparent, and thorough examination of this much debated issue to simply clear the air and provide scientific, objective evidence to argue a case for either position. As long as the issue is not openly addressed in a reasonable, logical manner, there will be confusion, dissent, and distrust.
- Some people feel there are very lonely priests who are lacking in a traditional domestic life and do not have the opportunity to be intimate with another human being. The need for closeness with another human being in some cases may become overwhelming. In some situations, these desires might turn sexual. This sexual searching might lead some priests to reach out to children in an inappropriate manner. Adequate research has not been done in this area. It is time to have outside, credible sources examine if unmarried priests are more likely to be pedophiles.
- In the same fashion, the impact that women priests might have on the role of the priest in protecting young children from being

molested should also be at least explored with an objective mind in a public forum.
- Serious consideration must be given to the collective personality of sexually offending priests. Almost every priest accused of sexual abuse within the Catholic Church, including Father Sylvestre, is extremely reluctant to ever admit that what he did was morally wrong. They blame the victim, downplay the harm done, and attempt to diminish the actual number of victims. Why do these convicted priests refuse to be remorseful and rarely express genuine guilt or sympathy for their young victims? Do they feel that, because they are ordained priests within the Catholic Church, they are somehow above the law and not subject to the same responsibilities? Why do many men become arrogant once they become ordained priests and feel that society must excuse, forgive, or forget their crimes even if they involve the abuse of young children? These questions need to be carefully examined; answers need to be provided.
- The Catholic Church needs to examine its collective soul and conscience and honestly ponder a very difficult question that, in many ways, lies at the very heart and soul of the matter. Would the Catholic Church ever have dealt with offending sexual abusing priests if parishioners, legal system, media, police, and victims themselves had not forced them to deal with the issue? The answer to that admittedly difficult and heart-wrenching question will go a long way to direct church committees in the method of dealing with future victims and situations. It is a question that must not be glossed over, answered with meaningless platitudes, nor ignored. It is one that must be addressed in an open-minded and serious light.
- The manipulation, marginalization, and, in some cases, absolute fabrication of the truth by the hierarchy of the Catholic Church with regard to sexual abuse issues within the church must be stopped. Priests, laity, and society as a whole must demand that this subterfuge finally end. The Catholic Church must demonstrate beyond a doubt that it is honest, truthful, and above suspicion. Any other approach damages the entire fabric of the Catholic Church and does nothing but provide enemies with justification for attacks.

- The Catholic Church must stop treating its sexually abusing priests as alcoholics. They have done this in many situations, including the early treatment of Father Sylvestre. There must be a recognition that sexually abusing clerics need specific and professional help designed to truly deal with their situation. The days of curing priests by superficial care and recovery by spiritual growth does not work. This inadequate response minimizes the problem and suggests a lack of real concern or care for their priests, victims, and parishioners.
- Funds should be allocated by individual dioceses to provide counseling for not only the victims of sexual abuse, but the perpetrators as well. Neither the victim nor the offending cleric should be cast aside to deal with the situation as best they can. Both need to be provided with help, guidance, and assurance there will be a professional agency assigned to help them with the rest of their lives.
- Cutting the victim or priest loose is no more acceptable than moving the offending priest to a new parish and pretending that nothing untoward ever happened. Only a qualified independent, professional can, with any degree of accuracy at all, evaluate offending priests and determine when and if a priest can be returned to normal parish responsibilities. Relying on church-appointed psychiatrists is not acceptable and should not be tolerated by the laity within the Roman Catholic Church.
- The church must stop looking under every nook and cranny for scapegoats when it comes to their priests who sexually abuse. It may very well be that the real problem does not entirely exist outside of the Catholic Church, but some responsibility has to exist within the church itself. Although a permissive world and a sensation-hungry media may have played a role, the issue of power, prestige, and privilege within the very structure of the church must be examined to determine if there is a connection. Is there something about the role, rights, and profile of a priest that attracts men who might be abusers?
- The Catholic Church must develop the necessary courage and fortitude to examine their modus operandi to determine if, in all of their practices, they are being true to the Gospel of Christ.

Or does their fear of prosecution and intense desire to promote a holier-than-thou image force them to instigate reforms based on legal advice? Do corporate lawyers or the innocent victims drive the church's response to sexual abuse cases? Gospel would seem to indicate that it is the vulnerable, weak victims who should dictate policy, but is it hijacked in some situations? The laity of the Catholic Church must clearly state its preference and act as watchdogs to ensure the Gospel of Jesus rather than the Gospel of Smoke and Mirrors and Public Opinion is being followed. With so many members in developing countries, the Catholic Church would do well to place a much clearer and more specific focus on the Catholic Church's social justice teachings.

- Catholic seminaries should properly, effectively, and critically screen all applicants to the priesthood, employing all of the modern psychological tools available. Many priests over the years have reportedly stated that sexual matters were never dealt with in a realistic, adequate, or helpful manner during their seminary years.
- Seminary curriculum should add programs dealing in psychosexual education. These courses should constantly be updated in order to keep pace with psychological advances. These courses should be mandatory for priests throughout their careers.
- Bishops and cardinals must be legally held responsible when they recommend inappropriate or questionable candidates for the priesthood when it is proven they had suspicions about their psychological makeup. In addition, action should be taken against those bishops and cardinals who ignore or refuse to take necessary action against priests who have been accused of molestation and other crimes.
- The Catholic Church should openly and publicly acknowledge the mistakes made so they are not repeated and so more lives (clerics and victims) are not lost to homicide and/or suicide.
- Bishops in every area touched by clerical sexual abuse must reach out to families in every parish, school, and institution so victims can get help, begin recovery, and report crimes to police for investigation, as Bishop Fabbro in the Diocese of London has done.
- Catholic bishops throughout North America must work with and lobby lawmakers for more and better laws that protect children

and vulnerable adults instead of actively undermining these laws by refusing to acknowledge the rights of sexual abuse victims in courts of law. Church officials should clearly demonstrate they are serious about preventing future abuse and help to bring healing and justice to those already harmed by abusive clerics and complicit bishops.

The average Catholic must study recommendations like the ones made here and demand the Catholic Church examine such concepts and take action on the ones they can. The average Catholic parishioner must quit being so submissive, obedient, and uninvolved. As a united and determined group, they must rise up and demand changes. They must insist on being given more power and refuse to be treated as unthinking, immature children.

Changes must be made within the very structure of the Catholic Church. It is the right and duty of all Catholics who love their church to demand they play a meaningful role in their church and participate as equal members. The power structure of the Catholic Church must change, or sexual abuse among its priests will continue despite the best intentions of caring priests, remorseful bishops, and outraged parishioners.

Conclusion

It is a time for a holy silence and a sacred listening.
Father Donald B. Cozzens, *Sexual Abuse in the Catholic Church*

As July 2007 heated up and the land lay parched and dry, the majority of Father Sylvestre's victims were still patiently awaiting word about final settlements from the Diocese of London. Meanwhile, in the faraway Archdiocese of Los Angeles, a storm that had been brewing for quite some time broke with a passion.

On July 16, 2007, the Roman Catholic Archdiocese of Los Angeles agreed to settle with an estimated five hundred plaintiffs for approximately $1.2 million each or between $600 and $650 million in total. This amount did not include an additional $114 million previously paid to another eighty-six victims in a prior settlement. Combining the two, it was by far the largest payout in the Catholic Church's history of sexual abuse scandals to date. As in the case of the Diocese of London, the Archdiocese of Los Angeles announced it was also selling off some of its properties to help finance these payouts. The news from Los Angeles was only the latest and largest of a number of huge payouts that have, since 2002, beset the Catholic Church in North America.

In 2004, the Diocese of Orange in California paid out $100 million to settle ninety claims. The Archdiocese of Portland in Oregon, recently settled with one hundred and seventy-five sexual abuse victims for $52 million and set aside another $20 million for expected future claims.

In 2003, the Archdiocese of Boston paid $84 million for five hundred and fifty-two victims. The Diocese of Covington in Kentucky settled their three hundred and sixty abuse claims for approximately the same amount. Dioceses in Tuscon, Spokane, Portland, Davenport, and San Diego have sought bankruptcy protection. (101)

If one wished to be a bit of a cynic, it could be argued that, if the Catholic Church does begin to purposefully examine its overall structure and make meaningful changes in policy, it will not be as the result of victims' tears nor books like this, but rather monetary concerns.

The payouts in the United States alone will very soon exceed $2 billion. The number of victims as well as the amounts paid continues to rise almost exponentially. It would seem that the need for changes within the church are obvious and can no longer, if only from a financial point of view, be denied, ignored, or sloughed off as a minor inconvenience that will soon melt away.

This book has taken a cursory, but well-documented look at the long history of abuse within the Catholic Church. It has examined the modern tidal wave of sexual abuse complaints in North America. This book has given voice to one particular victim who is symbolic of thousands of others. It has also attempted to give a glimpse into the life of one particular priest who abused and mirrored so many other offending clerics.

In its final analysis though, this book does not metaphorically throw up its hands and cast the Catholic Church off as yesterday's religion or as being irrevocably irrelevant. It instead offers hope through a series of what was meant to be thoughtful, relevant, pertinent, and helpful suggestions for the Catholic Church to consider as it rebuilds itself and hopefully rises like a phoenix from its ashes.

Draft Misconduct Policy

In June 2007, the Diocese of London came up with a draft sexual misconduct policy that was aimed at reassuring the faithful within the Catholic Church. In society as a whole, I suppose that other Father Sylvestres would not be allowed to wreak such pain and suffering upon the innocent again. The policy labels itself as a code of conduct for priests dealing with children and vulnerable people, and it includes a number of salient points:

- One-on-one religious instruction (between priest and child) is to be avoided.
- Confession with children is to be done in an open space in full view of others.
- Confession rooms are to be in high traffic areas; new ones will be constructed with clear glass openings.
- The two-deep rule (two adults must be present in dealing with children) must be implemented.
- Two adults must be present for recreational programs.
- A priest is never to take a person under nineteen on personal trips or vacations.
- Expensive gifts are not to be given to or accepted from a child, young person, or vulnerable person.
- Parents will be required to set reasonable boundaries in their relationships with others. For example, priests should limit counseling to three sessions.
- A priest is never to be alone with a child in his home or vehicle.

No one can argue with the good intentions behind the formulation of these policies. They must be commended as positive steps in the right direction. However, it remains to be seen how effective this policy will be and if it will actually be implemented on a day-to-day basis.

Will these positive steps be implemented in other dioceses, or will they just be reserved for the Diocese of London? The need for a uniform set of policies that are strictly followed throughout every diocese within the Catholic Church, at least in North America, is sorely needed. These policies, no matter how positive and forward-thinking they are, will still not address the systematic, hierarchical problems that exist within the universal Catholic Church that were discussed earlier.

The Pope Speaks

When news of the Archdiocese of Los Angeles settlement with its abuse victims became known, another announcement made worldwide headlines. Pope Benedict approved the release of a document that left liberal-minded Catholics, as well as many Jews and non-Catholic Christians, shaking their heads in disbelief.

In these precarious, gut-wrenching times with clerical sex scandals and church closings happening at alarming rates, the pope, confidently and boldly, reasserted the supremacy of the Roman Catholic Church and openly questioned the validity of any and all non-Catholic denominations.

After introducing a wider use of the old Latin mass, Pope Benedict sought to clear up what he had always regarded as "the erroneous interpretation" of Vatican II. He wanted to restate that "Christ established on earth only one church" and other religious entities cannot be called churches "in the proper sense" as they do not have "apostolic succession." He confidently stated the Catholic Church was "the only true path to salvation." (102)

If the pope was hoping to garner ecumenical sympathy from other religions for the sexual abuse scandals besetting dioceses in North America and, to a lesser extent, throughout the world, his efforts were severely crippled during one week in July.

Reactions from many Catholics and non-Catholics alike was immediate and, generally speaking, of one mind. Some saw it as insulting or arrogant; others wondered aloud how these statements jibed with professed Catholic doctrines of tolerance, love, and brotherhood.

In light of these pronouncements from the Vatican, it is difficult to perceive a time in the near future when the Roman Catholic Church, as a whole, would even superficially entertain the systematic, hierarchical suggestions made previously. It just seems that they are headed in a blind, right-wing direction with a damn-the-torpedoes approach.

One must seriously contemplate if these recent statements are indicative of a church that is now ready, as they approach several billion dollars worth of settlements, thousands of victims, and untold pain and suffering to truly evolve from a culture of silence, arrogance, and secrecy to one of conversation, consultation, collaboration, healing, and restoration.

If you read between the lines of this book, you will readily see that it is, in many ways, a desperate plea. It is a desperate plea that emanates from the victims, concerned Catholics, non-Catholics, lapsed Catholics, and all concerned citizens of the world. It is a heartfelt and earnest plea for the Catholic Church to pause and reflect upon what has happened to some of its priests and the little ones it has professed to love so much.

It is a time for the church as a whole to grieve, mourn, and partake in serious, thoughtful self-reflection, self-examination, repentance, forgiveness, and healing. It is not a time, I humbly submit, to assume a macho attitude that "my church is better than your church." It seems so absolutely adolescent, incongruous, and out of touch with reality.

It is rather a time for the Catholic Church to become the sane, logical, compassionate voice of these sexually abused victims who are, if one listens carefully enough, crying out for sincere apologies, heartfelt acknowledgement, and pastoral concern from the Catholic Church.

The Catholic Church now needs to assume the role of a humbler church, totally committed to serving the downtrodden, innocents, less fortunate, and wounded. Pope Benedict's July statements served to color the Catholic Church, in many people's minds, as arrogant, divisive, self-centered, and self-aggrandizing.

As it attempts to deal with what many are describing as "the worst crisis to ever face the Catholic Church," it should now be totally and absolutely committed to bridging differences, healing wounds, and joining other religions to form a powerful, ecumenical army intent on defeating sexual abuse in all aspects of life. The potential is there, and the time is right.

But maybe the reformation of the Catholic Church need not start nor should not begin with a pope, cardinal, bishop, or even parish priest. Maybe meaningful change and new directions for the future shall come from the parishioners. Maybe the laity of the Catholic Church will rise as one from their pews in North America and beyond and demand to take back what is, after all, their church.

Maybe it has been the average Catholic parishioner who has listened to the pleas and cries of the Lou Anns of the world and are shocked and embarrassed and now ready to take action. They no longer want to be part of an institution that refused to act, listen, and care for so many years.

Maybe it will be the person in the pews who will demand meaningful systematic and hierarchical change and will not take no for an answer. They are no longer the meek, mild, complacent, and malleable many who do what they are told by the few in Rome. They want a church that preaches as well as practices the Gospel they hold dear.

If not, then stories like Lou Ann and thousands of other sexually abused victims throughout the world will sadly echo through dioceses, churches, and cathedrals again and again in a litany of pain, suffering, and betrayal.

Endnotes

101) MSNBC.com, The Associated Press, "Settlement Represents Largest Payout In Sexual Abuse Scandal", July 14, 2007.

102) Chatham Daily News, "Pope Denounces Other Denominations As Not True Christian Churches", July 11, 2007.

The Final Word

Spring 2009 was, by southwestern Ontario standards, a cold, rainy, and rather depressing one. It seemed that winter was determined to hold on as long as possible before it relinquished its victims from its cruel grasp.

Set amidst this inhospitable season, a bright sun full of promise, hope, and warmth suddenly broke through the clouds one day in early May. Coincidentally, the warmth of spring arrived at approximately the same time that the London, Ontario, law firm of Ledroit Beckett Litigation Lawyers held a surprise press conference in which it was announced that the civil lawsuit involving Lou Ann Soontiens and the Roman Catholic Church had reached an amicable pre-trial settlement.

After five years of childhood sexual abuse, a related abortion, diagnosis with post-traumatic stress disorder, and decades of living with other effects of abuse, Lou Ann Soontiens received a measure of justice. The press conference was held on May 8, 2009, in the London, Ontario, offices of Ledroit Beckett Litigation Lawyers. With larger-than-life pictures of Father Sylvestre and a young, naïve Lou Ann Soontiens prominently displayed in the background and bracketed, the tearful, middle-aged Lou Ann Soontiens made statements and answered questions from a large crowd of reporters.

Lawyer Paul Ledroit formally began the press conference by announcing the Diocese of London had agreed to settle the civil lawsuit with Soontiens for $1.745 million dollars, plus legal costs.

It was estimated the final payout would be in excess of $2 million. (103) The agreement reached was believed to be the largest settlement involving an individual sexual abuse case in Canadian history, and it was reached only days before the commencement of the civil lawsuit trial was to begin on May 11, 2009.

Although some observers felt the settlement was larger than expected, lawyer Rob Talach of Ledroit Beckett clearly and correctly put things into perspective by stating, "The size of the settlement is indicative of the heinous nature of the abuse Soontiens lived through."(104) In addition, when one looks at the big picture of payouts by the Catholic Church with regard to sexual abuse cases in the United States, the amount awarded to Soontiens is not terribly out of line.

In 2003, the Archdiocese of Boston paid $85 million to over five hundred and fifty victims. In 2004, the Diocese of Orange in California paid $100 million dollars to settle ninety claims. In 2007, the Diocese of Spokane in Washington paid $48 million to settle about one hundred and fifty claims. The Diocese of Portland in Oregon agreed to pay $50 million to one hundred and seventy-five victims and set aside another $20 million for anticipated future civil lawsuits involving sexual abuse. In the same year, the Archdiocese of Los Angeles paid $660 million to over five hundred victims.(105)

The strategy of reaching an agreement with victims of sexual abuse shortly before civil trials can commence is also common strategy among Catholic dioceses in the United States as well. In July 2007, the Archdiocese of Los Angeles settled its five hundred and fifty clergy abuse cases the Friday before they were to go to court. In 2003, the Diocese of Vermont settled the first of two dozen clergy abuse cases against them the Friday before court was to begin on Monday.(106)

Shortly before going to trial in the civil suits involving over five hundred and fifty victims in the Archdiocese of Boston, an agreement was reached that halted the exposure of thousands of pages of church records on priests accused of sexual abuse. If these cases had gone to trial, it would have revealed a culture in which "top church officials within the Archdiocese of Boston coddled abusive priests and permitted them to molest again while stonewalling or paying off the victims of that abuse."(107)

Last-minute settlements by the Catholic Church in the United States can be spun many different ways by the various parties involved. When completing settlements literally hours before going to trial, church officials often explain their actions by expressing the desire to not put the victims through any more public suffering and pain.

Other observers, a little more cynical perhaps, cite the above-mentioned Archdiocese of Boston example and speculate the various church officials in the various dioceses involved do not want the extent, complicity, and duration of their involvement in these sexual abuse situations to be placed on public record and display in a trial usually quite well covered by the press.

According to Rob Talach, there was strong evidence that would have been brought to light in a trial, specifically that the Diocese of London "knew of Sylvestre's sexual perversions as early as 1953 (in Hamilton, Ontario) and did nothing about it." In addition, Talach said that, had this civil case gone to trial, "the abuse she [Soontiens] endured that took on every imaginable form and beyond would have made the trial very graphic and sensational."(108)

Reactions to the May 2009 settlement by the Diocese of London with Lou Ann elicited many different reactions, but most bloggers, responding to the news articles regarding the press conference, were quite supportive of Lou Ann, considering the amount she was given to be just, fair, and in line with her years of suffering.

One blogger identified as only as "Pennythoughts" compared the settlement to one given to Maher Arar, who was "imprisoned and tortured for just over a year and was ultimately compensated by the Canadian government with about $10 million while Lou Ann Soontiens received about $2 million for enduring years of sexual abuse."(109) Other comments posted directly addressed Soontiens (110):

- "You are an incredibly strong woman who has the power to heal the little girl inside." (Consuela, May 9, 2009)
- "I am also a survivor of abuse. Just know, Lou Ann, that God loves you as he does all of us. I will pray that you will once again believe." (Leni, May 9, 2009)
- "I was once proud to be Catholic, active in my church, but never again. My heartfelt prayers are with her and all others, men and

women, that were abused by these monsters." (Linda, May 9, 2009)
- "She should have gotten much more for what this monster did to her. What happened to the higher-ups in the church who knew what Sylvestre was doing but kept moving him from parish to parish?" (Frank, May 9, 2009)
- "A very sad story, no doubt about it. Interesting though how $1.75 million seems to take the pain away ... Sometimes I wonder if the real motive for all these commotions is justice or just money!" (SIL, May 9, 2009)
- "Cash for closure ... ridiculous!"(Mike, May 9, 2009)

The predominance of positive comments that surfaced immediately after Lou Ann's settlement provided a much-needed psychological boost for Lou Ann who, once she came forward with her accusations against Sylvestre, had to endure a number of cruel reactions over the ensuing years.

Snide comments, cold shoulders, and phone calls that accused her of attempting to close churches and being a money-grabbing bitch were not uncommon. In 2006, one woman came up to Lou Ann and, in all seriousness, said, "Thank God it was a priest who did it to you and not just a stranger off the street."(111)

Through it all, Lou Ann remained strong and resolute. Hours before her civil court case was scheduled to begin, her determination seemed to take on a steely edge and flourished. In an attempt to explain why she felt such resolve in facing such a daunting ordeal, she restated her commitment to taking it to the limit. "I wanted to let the public know what they [Catholic Church] did to me and to all those others and the sad fact that officials within the church could have stopped it but chose not to."(112)

After being awarded the settlement, Lou Ann felt not joy, but relief that all those years of suffering and having to endure the task of telling her story repeatedly to panels of church and insurance officials. She felt the money was not important. Rather, it was "the sense that someone listened to me and they believed me. For all those years I had to keep it inside and it gnawed away at me and eroded my sense of self." (113)

Lou Ann also saw the settlement as a ray of hope that her settlement would help others. Soon after receiving her settlement, she firmly and passionately restated her determination to stay involved with Sylvestre's other victims who have not yet settled and ensure they are able to obtain some form of closure and just reparation.

The Diocese of London, through their director of diocese communications, Mark Adkinson, handled the announcement of the settlement in a very carefully worded, seemingly sincere, and rather compassionate manner.

Adkinson contritely confirmed, "We [Diocese of London] are very sorry for all the hurt she [Soontiens] and others have experienced as a result of contact with Charles Sylvestre. All we can do is apologize, and we cannot apologize enough. People must remember that Charles Sylvestre is not the church."(114)

On the surface, some relatively impressive facts seemed to back up these positive comments. Since August 2006, more than fifty of the nearly seventy lawsuits filed by Sylvestre's other victims have been settled. Since January 2009, one claim has been, on average, settled each and every week by the Diocese of London.

However, it is not the sincerity of the Catholic Church's apologies, nor its desire to avoid future indiscretions by its priests, that is at the root of the overall problem. It is the difficulty that this massive, male-oriented, hierarchical corporation has in doing things in a different manner. It is a monolith of a ship that, once it starts heading in one direction, has great difficulty in stopping and charting a new course for the future.

The final word given by the Diocese of London and echoed repeatedly by countless other dioceses throughout North America in recent years was issued by Mark Adkinson on behalf of the diocese. Adkinson confidently and firmly stated, "We are doing everything we can to make sure something like this never happens again." (115)

We shall see.

Endnotes

103) Donald McCarthur, "Abuse Victim Wins Massive Settlement From Canadian Catholic Diocese", The Windsor Star, May 8, 2009.

104) CTV News, Victim of Abuse Awardred More Than $2Million", The Canadian Press, May 8, 2009.

105) MNSBC.com, "Settlement Represents Largest Payout In Sexual Abuse Scandal".

106) MNSBC. com, "Settlement Represents Church's Largest Payout In SExual Abuse Scandal".

107) Stephen Kujakin, 'Abuse In The Catholic Church", The Boston Globe, January 6, 2002.

108) CTV News, "Victim of Abuse By Priest Awarded More Than $2Million", The Canadian Press, May 8, 2009.

109) Pennythoughts Blog, "Bravo Lou Ann Soontiens", May 8, 2009.

110) All blogging comments taken from www.windsorstar.com/news/Priest+victim+gets/1577388/story.html.May 2009.

111) Author interview with Lou Ann Soontiens, February 2008.

112) Author interview with Lou Ann Soontiens, May 2009.

113) Author interview with Lou Ann Soontiens, May 2008.

114) Donald McCarthur, "Abuse Victim Wins Massive Settlement From Canadian Catholic Diocese".

115) CTV News, "Victim of Abuse By Priest Awarded More Than $2Million".

LaVergne, TN USA
23 April 2010
180358LV00002B/5/P